Settings for Slaughter

Settings for Slaughter

Thirteen Macabre Murders

DOUGLAS WYNN

ROBERT HALE · LONDON

© Douglas Wynn 1988
First published in Great Britain 1988

Robert Hale Limited
Clerkenwell House
Clerkenwell Green
London EC1R 0HT

British Library Cataloguing in Publication Data

Wynn, Douglas
    Settings for slaughter.
    1. Scenes of crime. Criminal investigation
    I. Title
    363.2′5

ISBN 0-7090-3529-2

Photoset in North Wales by
Derek Doyle & Associates, Mold, Clwyd.
Printed in Great Britain by
St Edmundsbury Press Ltd, Bury St Edmunds, Suffolk.
Bound by WBC Bookbinders Limited.

Contents

Acknowledgements

I should like to thank the Chief Constable of Lincolnshire and Detective Chief Inspector F. Ainsworth of the Lincolnshire Police for their assistance in my researches into the Major case. I should also like to thank Mr Cecil Maltby, Mr Len Turner and Mr Joe Kettleborough for valuable background information.

Thanks are also due to the librarian and his assistants at the Grimsby Public Library and to the staff of the local history sections of the following libraries: Leeds, Abertillery, Newport, Peterborough, Huddersfield, Oldham, Lincoln, Manchester and Carmarthen.

For permission to quote from Sir Patrick Hastings' book, *Cases In Court*, I am indebted to William Heinemann Ltd., London and for permission to quote from the *Poole and Dorset Herald* I thank the editor.

I also extend my grateful thanks to all the editors of the newspapers listed in the bibliography whose reports have assisted my research.

To my wife, Anne,
who had the original idea for the book
and helped in the research
but who died before it was finished.

Introduction

These stories of true-life murders are linked by a common theme. In each of the cases presented the location of the murder had an important part to play in the story. Thus the isolation of a farmhouse near Tadcaster allowed a murderer to subject two women to a night of terror. At another farmhouse, just outside Peterborough, the dilapidated state of the building enabled the police to bring a Fenland murderer to justice. Continuing the farming topic, the location of a farm in South Wales made it easy for a murderer to dispose of bodies and frustrated the police for weeks until a clever ruse by a Scotland Yard detective solved the case. In Cornwall possible riches hidden in a farmhouse provided the lure for a couple of tearaways intent on robbery with violence: the escapade ended in murder, yet the old place remained to frustrate their efforts to become rich quickly.

In contrast, the New Forest in Hampshire provided the right atmosphere for a private picnic and also for murder. The woodland area known as Cannock Chase, near Walsall, was conveniently placed near the home of a child murderer and gave the police many problems until a lucky break enabled them to bring him to justice.

The setting of the murder of a little girl in the close-knit community of a Welsh mining town had a marked effect on the investigation by the police, considerably impeding the efforts of the Scotland Yard men sent to track down the killer. Another town, this time by the seaside, provided a source of wealthy women preyed upon by a jewel thief whose burglary attempt ended in murder, and, in the case described, the town was able to supply a shingle beach for the handy disposal of the weapon.

The close proximity of a couple of village council houses led the tenant of one to spot a vital clue which led to the apprehension of a poisoner who otherwise would have got away with it. The scattering of houses on a hillside in the Pennines made it easy for a would-be burglar to observe when the occupants of a house went out, a circumstance which led directly to a double murder.

A hillside, this time near Huddersfield, was the setting of the brutal murder of two policemen, but the location may have contributed to the conviction and hanging of an innocent man. The wild hills above Glossop in Derbyshire, provided a perfect place for the disposal of a body and allowed a multiple murderer to avoid detection for a number of years.

Finally, the unlikely setting of a pub in Chesterfield enabled a killer to meet two of his victims.

1   Ernest Brown: The Lover's Revenge

'Well, I'm not going to mow the bloody lawn!' Ernest Brown's dark, handsome face was flushed with anger.

Dorothy Morton took a deep breath. She knew that it was now or never. In spite of her wildly beating heart, she tried to keep her voice calm. 'In that case I shall tell my husband you refused to obey orders.'

'It's not part of my flaming job. I'm supposed to look after the horses. And that's all I'm damn well going to do.'

'You're supposed to do anything my husband asks you to do. Or me for that matter, as I'm a director of the firm as well.' She took another breath. 'And if I tell him you've refused a reasonable order, you know he'll sack you!'

'It's not a blasted reasonable request. I'm a groom, not a gardener.'

She could see the rage rising in those hot, dark eyes. Then the dam broke. 'You can take your rotten job!' he shouted and the rest of the sentence was a string of obscenities. 'I'm leaving!' With that he strode away across the front lawn of Saxton Grange, then up onto the main road, and swung right in the direction of the Yorkshire village of Towton.

Dorothy Morton stood and watched him go. She

couldn't believe her luck. Ernest Brown, the bane of her life, was actually leaving. His fiery temper had finally got the better of him and accomplished what she had been unable to do.

As she went up the gravel drive to the road and stooped to pick some early June wild flowers from the grass verge, she could see his tall figure on the dusty road, and beyond him, a couple of miles away, the outlines of the village houses. She remembered the days when his arrogance and aggression had made him a romantic figure in her eyes.

It was three years ago, in 1930, when they'd had that never-to-be-forgotten day riding up onto the wild moors above Halifax. She'd been in her early twenties, he about thirty. Even though she'd been the mistress of her own riding school, and he was only the servant who looked after the horses, he had been able to sweep her off her feet. Her face burned as she remembered that summer's day when he had first overwhelmed her and made love in his typically tempestuous way.

For several weeks after that she seemed to live in a daze, unable to comprehend anything that was going on around her except for her beloved horses and the strong arms of her lover. But it was all too good to last. The passion of the man, which had first entranced, now began to irritate her. His constant demands, his impatience and, worst of all, his insane jealousy began to make her life a misery. The irritation grew to dislike, and the dislike to hate.

She tried to keep away from him as much as she could, but there were times when he would corner her in some barn or field, out of earshot of other people, and then he would force himself upon her. Sometimes he would threaten her with violence, and even inflict it, until she submitted to him. Afterwards she would be ashamed and angry with herself for having given in.

She constantly asked herself why she allowed this coarse and bad-tempered bully to dominate her in this way. Why didn't she complain to her husband? But it was the nagging fear of what Ernest Brown would do. He had often threatened to kill her if she refused him. And she couldn't get rid of a lingering feeling that sometime he would creep up behind her, and those powerful hands would fasten round her throat and choke the life from her body.

Frederick Morton, Dorothy's husband, came from a wealthy family of tar-distillers in Milnsbridge, near Huddersfield. Early in 1933 he took over two farms at Saxton Grange, some four miles from Tadcaster, which had belonged to his grandfather. The family, including Mr and Mrs Morton's two-year-old daughter, the baby's nurse, Ann Houseman, and Ernest Brown, moved to their new home.

Mrs Morton was not happy with the move, because the house, although a comfortable medium-sized farmhouse, was very isolated. It stood at the side of the main Sherburn-in-Elmet to Tadcaster road, but in those days the amount of traffic on it was small, and it was more than a mile to their nearest neighbours.

Ann Houseman lived in the house with them, but Brown had a hut on the farm. Although Mr Morton was frequently away, there were plenty of people about, working on the farm or in the office, during the day, but at night, apart from Mr and Mrs Morton, there was no one else at the farm but Ann Houseman and Brown.

Mrs Morton determined that she would stand up for herself, and soon an opportunity presented itself. The number of horses they owned had been reduced and there was not now the work for Brown that there had been. Mr Morton, after representations from his wife, decided to make the groom responsible for gardening as well, a job which he did not like. It was only a matter of time before the inevitable explosion occurred.

It was with relief that, when her husband came home that night, she was able to tell him of Brown's departure and ask him to obtain the services of another groom. He duly did so the very next day. But if Mrs Morton thought that she could get rid of the ex-groom quite so easily, she was in for a surprise.

That same day Brown rang her up and asked her to get him his job back. She refused. And when, in the next few days, she received a letter from him, again asking for reinstatement, she replied that it was out of the question.

The following Friday, when her husband was away on his usual trip to Carlisle and before the office staff had arrived, Brown appeared at the front door. She was so completely surprised to see him and overwhelmed by him that, when he threatened her, she promised to get him his job back.

The next morning Brown, having spent the night in his hut on the farm, appeared at the loose-boxes and assisted the new groom with the horses as if it were the most natural thing in the world. It seemed to Mrs Morton that he had gone back on the payroll without having been off it.

But the situation had not gone back to what it had been before. Dorothy Morton tried to keep out of Brown's way and would go near him only if she was sure someone else was present. The few times she did see the tall, dark man, his face had a sullen, bad-tempered look, and he always appeared to be arguing with someone.

As that hot summer slipped by, Dorothy Morton saw a lot less of Brown and was fully occupied with her riding school. Although her husband was often away in the evenings or came back too late to go anywhere, there was another car belonging to the firm, an Essex coupé, and in this she would go to the pictures in Tadcaster. Usually she went with friends, but it was not unknown for her to go to the pictures with just one man friend. On these occasions she didn't tell her husband who she had been with.

September arrived, but the hot weather which had been with them since early August showed no signs of abating.

Tuesday 5 September 1933 was warm and sunny. At about one o'clock in the afternoon Ernest Brown left Saxton Grange driving the horsebox containing a cow, bound for a farmer at Greetland, near Halifax. When he got there, the farmer decided that the cow wasn't the one he wanted and the ex-groom had to return it. He arrived back at the Malt Shovel Inn in Tadcaster, having stopped at a few pubs on the way, at just after eight in the evening.

Soon after Brown had left Saxton Grange that afternoon, Frederick Morton set off for Oldham in his Chrysler car. By 8.15 that evening he was back again, at the Boot and Shoe Inn at Peckfield, only some four miles from home.

Meanwhile, that afternoon Dorothy Morton had taken the Essex coupé to go swimming in the river at Wetherby. She was back in time for tea, and Ann Houseman then took the car herself. The nurse returned at about eight o'clock and left the car on the drive.

At about 8.30 p.m. Brown turned up with the horsebox. Mrs Morton was in the stackyard when he drove the large vehicle in, and the powerful headlights spotlighted her slim figure in the comparative darkness of the yard. Brown switched off the lights and swung down from the driver's cabin.

'Is the boss in yet? I want to see him about this cow.'

'No, he isn't.'

Brown walked to the end of the horsebox and opened the rear doors. The tailgate came down with a crash. 'What have you been doing with yourself today?' he asked.

Mrs Morton shrugged. 'Been swimming at Wetherby.'

'Go with anybody?'

It was at this point that Mrs Morton made her big mistake. Her next words transformed the quiet September evening into a night of terror which was to echo down the years.

'I've been with Mr … ,' she said, mentioning the name of a man with whom she was friendly and of whom she must have known Brown would be jealous.

There was a kind of stunned silence for a moment, then without saying anything further, Brown leaped forward and grabbed her by the shoulders. They were near the entrance to a barn, and he hurled her backwards into the opening so that she went down and banged the back of her head on the floor. It shook her up somewhat, but not enough to prevent her scrambling to her feet. She was able to dodge past Brown as he blundered towards her in the darkness of the barn.

'Ann! Ann!' she shouted as she raced past the horsebox towards the brightly lit opening of the kitchen door.

But Brown's legs were faster, and he caught her up as she was going by the end of the horsebox. Seizing her arms from behind, he swung her round and tried to force her towards the open end of the vehicle. But she broke free. Unfortunately he was now between her and the kitchen door, so she twisted round to pass on the other side of the horsebox.

The tall groom followed again, but this time, when he pounced, his hand reached for her throat. His long fingers wrapped themselves around her neck, and the awful nightmares she'd had of him coming up behind and strangling her seemed about to come true.

But the pressure on her neck was not increasing. He was simply pulling her along until they again reached the entrance of the barn. He pushed her roughly inside, and his voice was harsh as he hissed into her ear, 'I'll damn well finish you off, if you make another sound!'

Mrs Morton could not have made a sound, even if she had wanted to, but she stopped struggling, hoping that would placate him.

They heard the sound of footsteps in the yard. It could only be Ann. She must have heard Dorothy's cry and was coming to see what was the matter.

'Mrs Morton? Are you there, ma'am?'

Brown dropped his hands from Dorothy's throat and stood back. She could see the whiteness of his face in the gloom and could smell the alcohol on his breath. He'd been drinking. There was no telling what he might do. She must be very careful not to exacerbate the situation if she could help it.

She saw Brown put his finger to his lips as the shadowy figure of Ann Houseman came up to the entrance of the barn.

'I thought I heard you call me, ma'am?'

'No.' Mrs Morton's voice came croakily. 'I must have been calling to the cow.'

'Are you all right?'

'She's quite all right,' snapped Brown. 'And we don't need any help with the cow. You can go back inside.'

'I asked Mrs Morton,' said the nurse stubbornly.

'I'm quite all right, Ann. But I think we will go inside. Brown can manage the cow on his own.'

She didn't know how she managed to walk across the stackyard to the kitchen door. Her legs were trembling and her back was crawling with apprehension as any moment she expected to feel cold hands on her neck again. But Brown didn't seem to be following, and she could hear him clattering about, getting the cow out of the horsebox.

She and Ann went into the kitchen together and then up to the nursery to see if the young child was asleep. A short time later the nurse went downstairs into the kitchen in time to see Brown come in through the back door. His face looked grim, but he was quite polite as he said: 'Would you ask Mrs Morton if she could have a word with me?'

When the mistress of the house came into the kitchen, her face was pale. 'What do you want?' she asked. Her voice was unnecessarily high.

'I was wondering,' enquired Brown politely, 'if you could give me a hand with getting the ducks in? It needs two people, you know.'

'I know that but … I'm expecting a telephone call from my father any minute and I've got to stay in.'

Brown scowled and looked as if he would say something

more, but he didn't. He turned and went out of the back door.

Ann Houseman had earlier laid out Brown's supper on the large kitchen table, and she stood looking after him as he disappeared through the door. 'Presumably he'll be coming back for his supper?'

Mrs Morton shivered. 'I suppose so.' The near despair in her voice made the nurse look at her queerly. All Mrs Morton was hoping for at that moment was that her husband would come back. But she knew he was often late.

About half an hour later both women were startled by the sound of a gunshot just outside the kitchen window, and shotgun pellets rattled against the glass.

'What was that?' said Ann.

Mrs Morton shook her head, but her face had gone white. Then, as if driven by one accord, both women rushed out of the kitchen to the front of the house. Mrs Morton hid herself under the dining-room table, and Ann hid in the hall. But there was only silence from outside.

After some time, and when nothing further happened, both women thought that their positions seemed a little ridiculous and made their way back to the kitchen.

'Do you think Brown's gone mad?' asked the nurse.

'I wouldn't be at all surprised.'

'I suppose, if he comes back in, we'd better humour him until your husband gets back?'

'That's the best thing. But we'd better keep together.'

'I've been meaning to make some raspberry and apple jam.'

'That's a good idea. I've got some sewing to do.'

So, while Ann Houseman busied herself with her jam-making, Mrs Morton got out her sewing-box. Her hands were not very steady, however, and she had some difficulty threading the needle. Where on earth was her husband? Why didn't he come home?

Brown came in a few minutes later. He didn't look at the

women, and his face had a set, dangerous look about it. He went straight to the knife drawer in the big dresser which stood at one side of the kitchen and took out a white-handled game knife.

Mrs Morton, who was watching him out of the corner of her eye, drew a sharp intake of breath, then prayed that he had not heard her. She leaned her head down as if examining the stitches closely. But a sudden bang of the back door made her look up and she saw that Brown had gone out. Both women breathed a sigh of relief. They listened intently but could hear nothing from outside.

'What do you think he's up to now?' asked Ann.

Mrs Morton dumbly shook her head. Then she asked: 'Can you hear the sound of my husband's car?'

Ann listened carefully. She heard nothing.

'You'll only hear it on the road,' persisted Mrs Morton. 'When he comes down the drive, he switches the engine off so as not to disturb the baby, but you'll hear the sound of the wheels on the gravel.'

The nurse listened again, but she could still hear nothing.

The outside door opened again a few moments later, and in came Brown. He was carrying the white-handled knife and put it down on the dresser. He had that kind of closed-in look which was, if anything, more terrifying than his angry expression. But he did not look at the women and again went out.

It must have been around ten o'clock at night when Brown returned. This time he had a sporting gun under his arm. He looked at the two women and seemed about to say something. Both of them, seeing the gun, became very frightened.

It was the nurse who found her voice. 'Was that you shooting outside a while back?'

'I was shooting at some rats.'

'Rats? Why, it's dark outside.'

Brown said nothing. Mrs Morton recognized the gun as

one of her husband's. It was usually kept in the kitchen. Brown broke it open and extracted two cartridges. Mrs Morton noticed that one had been used but the other had not. He put them both in his pocket and then began to take the gun to pieces, carefully cleaning the inside of the barrel with the cleaning-rod. When he had finished, he put the pieces of the gun in a leather case and placed it in the cupboard in the kitchen where it was normally kept. Then he went outside.

It seemed to Mrs Morton that he couldn't seem to be still. He appeared to be driven by some inner force that would not let him rest. And she was afraid that he was building up to some sort of crisis.

Some time after this, both women heard the sound of wheels on the gravel outside.

'Was that the master's car?' asked Ann.

Mrs Morton nodded. She heard footsteps in the yard outside. The clock on the wall said 11.30. But she reminded herself that he had been later than this and had even been known to spend the night in his car in the garage.

The door opened. She raised her head. Brown came in. She kept looking, to see if her husband would follow him in, but he didn't. Brown shut the door behind him.

'Where's my husband?'

'What?' There was a puzzled look on Brown's face.

Mrs Morton repeated the question.

'The boss?' said Brown stupidly.

'That was his car out there a moment ago, wasn't it? We heard it on the drive.'

'Oh. Oh yes. It was the Chrysler all right. But he's gone out again.'

'Gone out again? But that's ridiculous. Why would he do that?'

'Don't ask me. He doesn't tell me things like that. I saw him come in and went to tell him about the cow. He just said: "All right". He's had a fair amount to drink, I could see that. Then I asked him if he wanted me to put the car away and he said, no, he was going out again.'

'But we didn't hear the sound of a car going up the drive.'

Brown just shrugged.

A terrible fear suddenly lurched in Mrs Morton's stomach. Brown must in some way have got rid of her husband. But she couldn't understand how. The gun was still in the kitchen, and she had heard no shot. And Brown had returned the knife to the dresser previously, so he couldn't have used that on her husband. In any case, there had hardly been time for much to have taken place, between the two women hearing the car and Brown coming in. Perhaps he hadn't killed Frederick after all. Possibly her husband had simply put the car away and gone to sleep in it, as he had before. And Brown had said he'd gone out again merely to frighten her. He was sitting down in the kitchen, and she tried to get on with the sewing.

'Do you want your supper?' asked Ann, but Brown merely shook his head.

Far from looking as if he'd just murdered someone, he seemed to be more lethargic than he had been, almost sleepy. His head began nodding, but every time Mrs Morton made a move, he lifted it. Finally she decided to try to end the stalemate.

She rose to her feet. 'I think I'm going to go to bed. Are you coming, Ann?'

Mrs Morton half expected that Brown would protest, but he didn't. 'If you're going to bed,' he muttered, 'I suppose I might as well go.'

After Brown left, Ann and Mrs Morton locked the door behind him and went up the stairs. Mrs Morton locked herself in the bathroom. She leaned her back against the door, and a wave of relief flooded over her. At least he couldn't get at her now. She couldn't resist putting the light out and going to the window which overlooked the farmyard but, peeping through the curtains, she could see nothing in the chasm of darkness below.

She must have stayed there, gazing out into the night, for nearly half an hour. Then she heard footsteps coming down the drive. For a wild moment she thought it might be her husband walking home, having had a breakdown in his car, but then she saw the shadowy figure of Brown coming into the yard.

He approached the kitchen door. Then he looked up. Mrs Morton drew back in case he could see her behind the curtains. She heard the sound of a key turning quietly in the lock and the whisper of the kitchen door being opened cautiously.

There came a sudden rustling in the corridor outside the bathroom and a hurried knock on the door, followed by a worried whisper from Ann Houseman.

'Mrs Morton!' Dorothy opened the bathroom door. ''Ma'am, I think Brown's coming into the house!'

They could hear the sound of footsteps softly crossing the kitchen.

'What shall we do, Ann?'

'Come into my bedrom. We shall be near the child, and we can close the door.'

The soft thud of feet on the stairs came towards them.

The two women quickly crossed the landing, went into Ann's room and shut the door behind them. The baby occupied the same room, but she seemed to be sleeping peacefully.

There was silence outside as the two women sat on the bed in the darkness, shivering with fright. They heard the creak of the stairs begin again. Another long silence. Then the sound of footsteps on the landing, right outside their door. They sat like statues, hardly daring to breathe, clasping each other's hands. There was no sound from outside the door.

How long they waited, they couldn't guess, but it seemed like hours. They both realized that it must now be the early hours of the morning. Then there was the faintest of sounds. It was the creak of a stair. But it seemed to come from a long way off. Then the muffled sound of a footfall. But it came from beneath them. Suddenly the truth dawned on them.

Brown was leaving.

Neither moved for quite a long time, scarcely daring to believe that the danger had passed. Then there came two small explosions from outside, followed by a crackling noise.

'That sounds like fire,' said the nurse, and she went to the window. 'It is! Come and look.'

Mrs Morton went to the window. By this time she could hear the fire and smell the smoke. Flames were shooting up from the garage, and the drive was lit up with the glare. The horses were making terrified noises in their loose-boxes, and from further along came the sound of frightened cattle.

'My God! He's set the place alight!' cried Dorothy. 'We'd better phone for the fire brigade.'

Together they rushed downstairs. But on picking up the phone they found that it was dead. They could hear the flames more closely now and smell the smoke seeping into the house.

'We shall have to get out, Ann, before the place burns down. You go up and get the baby. I'll get some rugs.'

A few minutes later they rushed out of the front door, on the side of the house away from the flames.

'We'll hide by the front hedge,' said Mrs Morton, 'cover ourselves with the rugs, and with luck he won't be able to see us.'

They crept up the garden and hid under the hedge. The house was now silhouetted against the flames which seemed to be threatening to engulf it at any moment. Mrs Morton was thankful that Brown had released the horses and cattle. She could hear the clattering of their hooves on the gravel.

Then she heard Brown's voice: 'Mrs Morton! Mrs Morton!'

'Keep down, and try to keep the baby quiet.'

Brown came round the corner of the house, and, seeing the front door open, went in, still calling for the mistress. The two women crept away through the orchard to make their way across the fields in the direction of Towton.

It was only when they had gone some way across the fields that Mrs Morton realized that, if her husband had indeed gone to sleep in the Chrysler and Brown had set fire to the garage, it looked like a deliberate attempt to kill him.

They heard the sound of the horsebox being started up at the farm, and a short time later it passed on the road, going in the direction of the village. Mrs Morton guessed that Brown would be going to the house of the farm manager, Murray Stewart, who lived in Towton.

Brown knocked up Stewart, and together they went to the farm and then on to the next village to inform PC Broadhead and phone for the fire brigade. During the drive Brown said that he'd seen his boss come in at 11.30 and had offered to help him put his car away, but that Morton had said he might be going out again. He never saw Morton go out but, after he'd gone to bed, he heard the car being shunted about.

When the fire brigade arrived at the farm, they found that the fire was confined to the barn which was used as a garage. Its roof had collapsed and the building was still burning. They finally extinguished the flames at about nine o'clock in the morning and then discovered that there were the all but destroyed shells of two cars in the burnt-out building. One of the cars inside was pulled out with the aid of a tractor.

In what was left of the seat next to the driver's, PC Broadhead made a macabre discovery. He found what he afterwards described as a charred lump, which appeared to be human flesh. By some rings which were found on and near the body and by some keys, it was identified as being the remains of Frederick Morton.

When later the two cars were examined by experts, it was discovered that the petrol-tank draining-nuts were missing. This led the police to suppose that the tanks had been opened by removing the nuts, and when a sufficient amount of petrol had run out underneath, it was ignited deliberately, causing the fire. A pair of pliers which were known to belong to Brown were also discovered in the garage.

Dr Sutherland, County Pathologist, conducted the post-mortem and found that the legs had been burned away below the knees. Part of the arms were missing, and so was part of the skull. The remaining portion was only some thirty inches long, and it included some of the trunk and thighs. The best-preserved portion, however, was near the stomach and, although it was badly charred, it was still possible for the pathologist to detect a gunshot wound.

In fact, he recovered some cardboard wadding from the cartridge and some shotgun pellets. These pellets enabled a gun expert to show that they were of the same type used for the gun kept in the kitchen. When the shotgun which Brown had been using and had put away in the kitchen was examined, minute bloodstains were found on the outside of the barrel. They were shown to be human blood.

The police surmised that Morton had been shot at close range, probably when he was getting out of the car. They showed that from the kitchen it was almost impossible to hear a gun being discharged in the garage. It was most likely that the farmer did not come home at 11.30 as Brown had suggested. At that time Brown was probably merely putting away the Essex car which Ann Houseman had left in the drive. But when the women heard the noise of the wheels on the gravel and assumed it was Mr Morton coming home, Brown went along with the idea.

What probably happened was that the farmer came home at about nine o'clock and ran the car down the drive without the engine, as was his custom. The women in the house simply didn't hear him. But Brown did and, after an argument in the garage, shot Morton as he was getting out of his car. Brown then ejected the cartridge and threw it into a field, where it was afterwards discovered. He replaced the cartridge with a new one and discharged the gun near the kitchen window in case the women had heard the first shot, so he could then claim he was shooting rats.

He realized that the women might phone for help, so he took the knife from the kitchen drawer and severed the telephone wire where it ran up the outside wall of the house. Microscopic examination of the cut ends of the wire and of the blade of the knife showed that the wire had actually been severed by the white-handled game knife which Brown had taken from the kitchen.

A coil of rope was afterwards found on the landing outside the bedroom in which the women had sought shelter. There is little doubt what Ernest Brown would have used the rope for, if he had managed to get Mrs Morton on her own during that night of terror.

In the event, at the West Riding Assizes held in Leeds in December 1933, a jury took just an hour to find him guilty of the murder of Frederick Morton and it was Brown who received the rope.

2   Harold Jones:
A Child Goes Missing

'Where on earth is young Freda?' asked George Burnell.

'I don't know,' said his wife. 'Didn't you send her down to Mortimer's for some spice?'

'Some fowl spice and some grit,' corrected her husband. 'I gave her tuppence ha'penny for the spice and a shilling for one of those seven-pound bags of grit. And the little madam had the nerve to ask me for pocket money for going! So I said that if she was quick I'd give her a penny. It should have taken her ten minutes at the most, but that was nearly an hour ago and I'm waiting to feed the chickens.'

The little Welsh town of Abertillery lies in a steep-sided valley some fifteen miles from Newport. In 1921 coal mines lined the floor of the valley, and the houses climbed the hillside to the east, the terraced rows running parallel with the River Ebbw below. One of those rows was Earl Street, the home of eight-year-old Freda Burnell, and another was Somerset Street in which was Mortimer's Corn Stores, where the little girl had been sent, that cold Saturday morning in February.

When Freda hadn't returned in an hour, Mr Burnell went looking for her. He passed Mortimer's shop, looking

through the half-glass street door to see if she was inside. Then he went on to the Co-operative Stores, but she wasn't there either. He returned home feeling a mixture of anger and apprehension.

When she didn't come home for her midday meal, her parents became more worried still. Friends and neighbours began searching the streets of the little town, where news of the disappearance spread quickly. At 1 p.m. her father went to the police.

At 6.30 that evening there came a knock on the door of the Burnell house. It was opened by Mr Burnell. Out in the street stood a heavily built young man who looked considerably older than his fifteen years. He worked as a delivery boy for Mr Mortimer and occasionally helped out in the shop.

'Just thought I'd enquire about Freda, see if she's turned up yet. Some people came in the shop earlier, said she was missing. You see I served her this morning.'

'What time was that?'

'Oh, it would be sometime after nine. I get to the shop, see, at just after nine. I usually come in the back way, into the kitchen, then go upstairs and open the shop door. Well, I'd just done that this morning and gone back downstairs to get some coal to light the fire in the shop stove, when the servant told me there was someone in the shop. So I went back upstairs, and it was Freda.'

'Know her by sight, do you?'

'She sometimes comes to play with my sister Flossie.'

'Oh yes, I know you. You're Harold Jones, and you live in Darran Road, don't you?'

'That's right. Well, Freda asked for a packet of spice and a bag of grit. I served her with the spice, see, but said we hadn't got any grit in bags. She left the shop, and that's the last I saw of her.'

'It's very kind of you, Harold, to come and tell us. We haven't seen her all day, and her mother's getting very worried about her.'

The search for the little girl had gone on all that day. The services of the town crier had been obtained, and he had toured the locality asking for information about the missing child. But it was in vain. The police took up the search in the afternoon and evening, and search-parties of police and civilians scoured the surrounding woods and hillsides. In the darkness of the early February evening the lights of the miners' lamps could be seen criss-crossing the moors where the men were searching. But nothing was found.

The next day was Sunday 6 February. At half-past seven, just as dawn was breaking, Edward Lewis, who looked after the pit ponies at the Navigation Colliery, came out of his back garden gate to go to work. He lived at 7 Duke Street and stepped out into the narrow lane which ran between the back of Duke Street and the back of Princess Street. Almost immediately he saw, further up the lane, the huddled-up body of a little girl. She was lying on her side, feet towards him, close to the wall which marked the edge of the lane.

He needed no telling who it was, for the whole town had heard of Freda Burnell's disappearance, and he rushed up, thinking the poor child must have got lost and sunk down exhausted during the night. When he reached her, he realized his mistake, for her legs and hands had the coldness of death. Then he saw that her legs were tied together with string just above her boots, her arms bound behind her by the elbows, and her muffler was wound tightly round the lower part of her face and neck. He left her there and quickly called the police.

The Deputy Chief Constable of Monmouthshire, Henry Lewis, who was also the Superintendent of the Abertillery Police, was soon on the scene. He noticed that on the clothing of the little girl there was chaff, and there was also chaff on the ground beside and underneath her. He came to the conclusion that the body had probably been carried from somewhere else in a sack which had contained chaff.

Dr Simon Simons examined the body soon after it had

been taken to the little girl's home and later performed an autopsy. He found that her face and forehead were bruised, suggesting that she had been struck on the head with some hard object. Her petticoat had been ripped at the front, and her knickers undone at the back and also torn. There was evidence that someone had made an attempt to rape her. Freda's scarf had been wound tightly round her neck in what may have been an attempt to stifle her cries but which had resulted in partial strangulation.

The doctor found the actual cause of death hard to establish and eventually put it down to shock caused by a combination of factors: the attempt at rape, the partial strangulation and the blow on the head. He suggested that the time of death was about 1.30 on Saturday afternoon.

The presence of chaff suggested that the body had been in some sort of barn, and several barns on farms around the town were examined – without success. By Monday the police were getting no further, and at midday the Chief Constable asked for the assistance of Scotland Yard. At ten o'clock the next day Chief Detective Inspector Albert Helden and Detective Sergeant Alfred Soden alighted at Abertillery station.

Enquiries made among the residents of Duke Street and Princess Street, whose back yards were near where the body was found, soon produced several people who had heard the scream of a child that Saturday. They all put the cry at about 9.30 in the morning.

'That means,' said Superintendent Lewis, 'that she was attacked somewhere along the lane, then taken away and kept possibly in a barn on a farm somewhere, killed about midday and the body brought back on Sunday morning.'

'I don't think so, sir,' replied Chief Inspector Helden. 'It's quite possible the little girl was attacked at 9.30, rendered unconscious and yet did not die until several hours later. She could have been assaulted in a shed or hut not very far from the lane and simply left there to die, then afterwards dumped in the lane nearby.'

'Of course,' said the Superintendent, 'Mortimer rents a shed around there, somewhere. He's a seed merchant and uses it as a store-house. That would account for the chaff.'

It was evening before they visited the shed. It stood in the back yard of 106 Princess Street, the home of Mrs Evans, and had a door which opened directly onto the lane where the body had been found. Another door in the shed opened onto Mrs Evans's yard, while the yard itself had a gate which also led onto the lane. The shed had a boarded-up window overlooking the yard. Superintendent Lewis, Chief Inspector Helden, Sergeant Soden and PC Cox searched the small building. Inside they found a chicken run with chaff on the ground inside it, and also chaff on the floor of the shed. There were sacks and boxes piled on each other, and on one wall there was even a water tap.

After about ten minutes searching by the aid of lanterns and torches, Sergeant Soden gave a shout: 'Over here!'

The others crowded round where he was standing, just behind the door. There, under some boxes, was the white corner of a handkerchief. They carefully pulled it out.

'It's plainly a child's handkerchief,' said the Chief Inspector. And he was right. It was afterwards identified as belonging to Ivy Burnell, Freda's sister. It was known that they borrowed each other's handkerchiefs.

Helden went back to talk to Harold Jones, who had already been interviewed several times before, as he was the last person to have seen Freda alive.

'I understand one of your duties was to feed the chickens in Mr Mortimer's shed. You were supposed to feed them in the morning, between nine and ten, at dinner time and then again at tea-time?'

'I didn't always feed them three times a day,' said Harold defensively. 'I didn't feed them in the morning on that day.'

'So you didn't go to the shed at all that morning?'

'I didn't say that. I had to make a delivery with the cart

at about ten o'clock, and coming back I went to the shed for a sack of potatoes.'

'Did you see anything unusual in the shed?'

'Nothing at all.'

'Anybody with you?'

'Young Frank Mortimer, Mr Mortimer's son. He sometimes helps me on a Saturday.'

'And he came into the shed with you?'

'No, he didn't. I told him he could either hold the cart or help me with the sack, and he decided to stay with the cart. The other week some boys ran off with it, see?'

'Tell me what you did the rest of the day.'

Harold Jones explained that he had spent some time working at the shop, gone home to dinner and then served in the shop until four o'clock, when he went to feed the chickens in the shed.

'And did you notice anything different this time?'

The boy took his time answering, then shook his head. But it was obvious to the chief inspector that the young man was holding something back.

'Come on. There's something else. Out with it!'

Harold looked uncomfortable. 'Promise you won't tell Mr Mortimer?'

'Look here, young man. You'll be in very serious trouble unless you answer all my questions truthfully. Now I'll ask you once again. There's something else you haven't told me, isn't there?'

'I left the shed unlocked.'

'You did what?'

'I'm supposed to lock it up behind me when I leave and put the key back on its nail in the shop. But I must have forgotten. And then later that evening, when I was walking along Princess Street with Teddy – that's Edmund Clissett, you see, suddenly I thought about the key. I couldn't remember putting it back on its hook, so I went back, and there it was still in the lock. But you won't tell Mr Mortimer I left the shed unlocked, will you?'

'What time was this?'

'About half-past ten.'

'Let's get this straight. The shed was actually unlocked from four o'clock, when you went to feed the chickens, until 10.30 at night, when you went back to look for the key?'

The young man nodded miserably and confessed that he had carried the key with him until he had put it back in the shop on Monday morning.

His story was confirmed by seventeen-year-old Edmund Clissett, who said he had gone to the shed with Harold Jones and had actually been inside it. The shed was dark until Harold struck a match, and he had seen no sign of the girl's body there. This was supported by the evidence of several other lads who had also gone along to the shed with them but had waited outside in the lane.

'They're lying!' snapped the Chief Inspector when later he and the Superintendent discussed the case.

The Welsh policeman shrugged his shoulders. 'You've got to be careful with these people. They're a close-knit Welsh community, and they don't take kindly to English policemen from Scotland Yard coming down here and trying to bully them.' When Helden protested, Lewis went on: 'You asked Clissett, who's only seventeen, if he'd like to spend a night in the cells, and told him that if he didn't tell the truth he would stand beside Harold Jones in the dock.'

The Scotland Yard man compressed his lips. 'I believe Harold Jones is guilty.'

'Well, you haven't got a very strong case against him. According to witnesses, the little girl's scream was heard near the shed at 9.30. Yet Mortimer claims he was in the kitchen from 9.15 to 9.40, except for a short time when he went to wash, and he could hear Jones upstairs in the shop the whole time.'

'He could have been mistaken about the times.'

'Doesn't give the boy much time, though, to serve the

girl in the shop, take her up to the shed, which is quite a few minutes walk away, murder her there and come back.'

'That, sir, is what I believe happened,' said the Chief Inspector stolidly.

'And how did he get rid of the body?'

'I think the body was there all the time during the day, probably already in a sack. He said that young Frank Mortimer did not want to come into the shed with him, but it would have been easy to persuade the boy to stay outside. Then there was a gap in Clissett's testimony of the evening proceedings. They had been at his house, and Jones left to go home. Later Clissett went up to Jones's house to borrow some playing-cards and met Jones, who said he'd been to the fish shop. In that gap Jones could have removed the body and dumped it in the lane.'

'But several people went up and down that lane subsequently, one of them a policeman, and none saw the body.'

'It is a very dark lane, and at night, with the body close to the wall, it might be possible to miss it.'

Superintendent Lewis expressed his disbelief with a single explosive sound. 'The fact is, Chief Inspector, that you haven't a very good case. And there is a great deal of popular support for the boy in the town. Whether it leads witnesses to tell lies, I don't know, but it does mean we've not got the backing I would like. And if this pit strike there's all the rumours about takes place, the police are going to be even less popular than they are now.'

The Scotland Yard man's face was grim. 'There's a lot of circumstantial evidence against Jones – enough, I would have thought, to charge him. And I should like you to consider the situation, sir. This was a savage, unprovoked attack on a little child. I wouldn't want to risk its happening again.'

'And neither would I. All right, then. The Chief Constable has put you in charge of the case. If you want to charge the boy, go ahead. But I'm not happy about the outcome.'

In the event the Deputy Chief Constable was right.

The trial began in the Shire Hall at Monmouth, on Monday 20 June, by which time the pit strike had started. Mr Justice Bray presided, with C.P. Vachell KC prosecuting, and the prisoner was defended by J.B. Matthews KC.

Harold Jones was given an alibi for the time of the murder, not only by his employer, Mr Mortimer, but also by Mrs Mortimer and the servant girl. All three had been in and around the kitchen at the relevant time and said that they had heard the boy upstairs in the shop.

Mr Mortimer even went so far as to take part in an experiment. He and the defending solicitor, Mr Everett, an Abertillery man, showed that it was possible to reach in through the window of the shed and throw a handkerchief onto the floor so that it landed in approximately the position in which little Freda Burnell's had been found – showing that the evidence could have been planted afterwards by almost anyone. In vain did the police claim that the window was securely boarded up when they first saw it and that there was no gap through which any object could be thrown. Mortimer's evidence obviously left a doubt in the minds of the jury.

In addition a witness was found who had been along the lane some twenty minutes before the body was discovered and who claimed not to have seen it. But he also said that he'd seen a strange man standing near where the body was afterwards discovered. And he'd never seen the man either before or since.

Harold Jones's demeanour must also have impressed the jury. Dressed in a smart blue suit and looking composed and self-confident, he gave his evidence calmly and could not be shaken by the prosecuting counsel.

The trial created a sensation in the area, and large crowds collected outside the Shire Hall on each of the four days of the trial, rushing for seats when the doors were opened. On the last day the jury took an hour and twenty-five minutes to find Harold Jones 'not guilty'. Such were the excitement and popular support for the boy that, even before the foreman of the jury rose to give the unanimous verdict, the judge had to warn the public against any demonstration in court.

But outside it was pandemonium. When Jones was released and appeared in the street, he was surrounded by an ecstatic throng shouting and cheering. He and his family were followed to a neighbouring hotel where they were staying. Outside, the noisy crowd remained until eventually the boy, like some royal prince, appeared on the hotel balcony and addressed them. 'I thank you all,' he said.

The 1920s were characterized by some very hot summers, and the month of July 1921 was a scorcher. On Friday the 8th – even on the high hillside of Abertillery and in Darran Road, which is so high up the hill that it overlooks most of the town – it was still warm at 9.30 at night.

Outside her home, at number 4, played eleven-year-old Florence Little. She was with her friend Flossie Jones, the sister of Harold Jones, who lived further along, at number 10, and Florrie's younger sister, seven-year-old Lily May. They were playing hopscotch.

At a little after 9.30 p.m. Florence Little's mother came out to call her children in for bed. Lily May was sitting on a doorstep opposite.

'Where's Florence?'

'She's gone to Flossie Jones's.'

Mrs Little walked up the street to number 10. The door was shut, which was unusual, for in that heat most people left their front doors open. She tried it, but it was locked. She knocked, but there was no reply. She knocked again. Eventually, after a delay of several minutes, she heard the bolts being drawn and the door opened a little. In the semi-darkness inside she could make out the stocky, muscular figure of Harold Jones. He had only a pair of trousers on, tied at the waist with braces.

'Sorry to be so long, Mrs Little, but I was having a bath.' In his hand, Mrs Little noticed, he was carrying a hairbrush.

'Is Florence inside, playing with Flossie?'

'No, she isn't. She was here, but she went out the back way.'

Mrs Little went away and questioned Lily May again. The child said she had heard Flossie Jones tell Florrie that Harold wanted her, and the two girls had gone into the Jones' house. Flossie Jones soon came out, but Lily May did not see her sister leave.

This in itself was not all that worrying, for it was possible to get out the back way, and the girl might have gone into another street. Nevertheless, Mrs Little hung about in the rapidly darkening road, asking if anyone had seen her daughter.

She saw some people coming up from town – Mr and Mrs Jones and the lodger, William Greenway – and asked them if they'd seen her daughter.

A lost child would not ordinarily cause many misgivings but, coming as it did so close to the murder of little Freda Burnell, it was the cause of much comment. Mr and Mrs Jones closely questioned their son when they reached home, but he merely repeated what he had told Mrs Little. He also said that, in having a bath, he had dropped his shirt and got it wet, and he asked his mother for a clean one. Then he went out to help with the search for Florrie Little.

The police were called and began a search of gardens and streets and the high moor at the back of the small town. Philip Jones, Harold's father, helped in the search, and neither he nor his wife went to bed at all that Friday night.

At 8.45 the next morning Mr Jones was sitting in the back kitchen with his wife while Harold was out with his friends. There came a knock at the front door, and on the doorstep stood Superintendent Lewis and PC Cox.

'We are searching all the houses along here,' said the Superintendent. 'I wonder if you'd mind if we searched yours?'

'Not at all. Come in, by all means.'

They searched downstairs, then went upstairs. They looked through the back bedroom, which was Harold Jones's room, then came out again onto the landing. The Superintendent looked up and saw a manhole in the ceiling. 'Ah, I see you have a fanlight. Can we get up there?'

'Yes. I'll get a chair.'

While Mr Jones was fetching a chair from Harold's bedroom, PC Cox asked: 'Do you see the wall over there by the manhole cover? It looks to me as if someone's tried to wash it.'

Superintendent Lewis nodded. 'There's also a faint dark stain by the side of the manhole cover,' he replied.

When the chair was brought, PC Cox, who was taller than the Superintendent, mounted it. He pushed up the cover, hauled himself up and flashed his torch through the hole.

'It's here!' he shouted. 'It's here!'

A few moments later the child's body lay on the landing. Her clothes were saturated with blood. A man's grey army shirt had been wrapped round her head and neck, and the little girl's throat had been cut. The police later found a large clasp knife, heavily stained with blood, in the kitchen drawer. There were also clots of blood in a saucepan which had been placed under the leaking outlet pipe from the low sink. It was surmised that the child had been attacked in the kitchen and her throat cut while she was being held over the sink. Then the body was taken upstairs and hoisted up into the loft by means of a piece of rope which was found underneath the girl's arms.

Philip Jones staggered out of the house. He walked a few streets and found Harold calmly sitting on the windowsill of a shop, talking to some friends.

'Come here, sonny.' Harold got off the sill and approached his father. 'They've found the body in our house,' continued Mr Jones.

'I never done it, Dad.'

'You or me will have the blame. Come and face it.'

When word got round that Harold Jones had again been charged with the murder of a little girl, an angry crowd surrounded the police station. Such was the popularity of the boy and the opprobrium in which the police were held at the time that it wasn't until Superintendent Lewis came out to tell them that the body had been found in Harold Jones's home that they agreed to disperse.

This time there was very strong evidence linking the boy with the murder of the little girl. He had been seen to go into the house with her and was alone until his parents came home an hour or so later. A witness was found who had been near the back door and could swear that the girl had not come out that way. And the murder had plainly been committed in the house.

Harold Jones's legal advisers were in something of a difficulty. The boy would be sixteen years old the following January, and it was already July. If he pleaded 'not guilty' – which is the normal course of action at a murder trial, the preparations for the trial could well take it into the New Year. Then, if he was found guilty, he would be hanged. Whereas, if he was only fifteen, the sentence would be to be 'detained during His Majesty's pleasure'.

Harold Jones pleaded guilty to the murder of Florence Little at the trial, which opened on 1 November 1921. During his stay at Usk Gaol, near Newport, before the trial, and at the instigation of the prison chaplain, he wrote a full confession. He also confessed to the murder of Freda Burnell.

3   John Williams:
The Case of the Hooded Man

In the winter, seaside resorts might seem quiet places, inhabited only by the folk likely to be found in any small town, but in 1912 some of the resorts along the South Coast were not like that at all. Eastbourne, for example, had an almost permanent population of wealthy residents who stayed on well into the winter.

One of these was the Countess Sztaray, the daughter of a Hungarian nobleman. An elderly lady, she was well known in the town for her good works and also as the possessor of some valuable jewellery.

On the night of 9 October the Countess ordered a cab to take her to a function at an hotel in the town. At 7.15 David Potter, the coach-driver, arrived at 6 South Cliff Avenue, a house with a projecting entrance way and a narrow front garden space. He was driving a single-horse brougham and had come early because he knew that the Countess did not like to be kept waiting. He settled down in his seat to enjoy a quiet pipe.

There was a wooden balcony over the front door, and in the gloom above it Potter thought he saw a faint movement. He blinked and then, as his eyes became more used to the darkness, he could just make out the head and shoulders of a man.

The front door opened suddenly, and light splashed down the path to the front gate and the pavement beyond. Potter could see no more of the figure on the porch. He hurriedly got down from his seat as he heard the Countess's voice.

'It's Potter, isn't it? Why, you are a stranger!' She strode down the path with her companion, Mrs Fuller, following behind.

The coachman eased off the brake, and they clattered down the hill, away from the sea, towards town. At the bottom of the street he turned right, into Silverdale Road, then pulled in to the kerb and leaned over to speak to the Countess. 'Your ladyship, there's a man lying on top of your balcony.'

'The devil there is! Why on earth didn't you say so earlier? Drive back immediately.'

Potter knew better than to argue with her ladyship. He turned the brougham round in the road and drove back up the hill, stopping outside number 6 South Cliff Avenue. The Countess, after a cursory glance up at the balcony, marched up the path to the front door.

She telephoned the police station at the town hall. PC Luck took the call and in turn telephoned the Parade office along the front with the message that there was someone lying on the porch of the front door and it was thought that he might get in through the bedroom window on the first floor. Inspector Walls, who took the call, said he would go at once.

Potter, sitting on the brougham, was beginning to wish he was somewhere else, and it was with great relief that he heard the sound of footsteps coming down the hill from the direction of the sea and was able to make out the uniform of a policeman. He gave a low whistle to attract the policeman's attention.

'Is that number six?' asked Inspector Walls, coming across the road.

Potter nodded and the Inspector went past him and up the drive to the front door. It was opened by Mrs Fuller, who pointed silently upwards with her finger.

The policeman stepped back into the drive and, shading his eyes with his hand against the glare of the hall light, looked upwards.

'Now then, my man. Just you come down.'

The man above the door appeared to lift himself into a sitting position, and the Inspector moved to the right to receive him when he climbed down. Suddenly there was a flash and the crack of a pistol shot from above the balcony. The policeman clutched the left side of his chest and almost went down, then began staggering back through the gate.

The report frightened the horse, which shied, so Potter took the opportunity of putting some distance between himself and the gunman. He urged the animal into a gallop up the hill. He didn't look back and so didn't see the Inspector collapse on his face in the roadway.

Potter turned left out of the avenue into South Cliff and then down the hill towards the Grand Parade, finally stopping at the cab rank there. He told a colleague what had happened, and together they made their way back to South Cliff Avenue.

When they arrived, a small group of people were already gathered around the police inspector, who was stretched out on the pavement. He had been moved from the roadway and turned over so that he now lay on his back. His tunic had been opened to reveal a wound in his left breast, which was bleeding freely. A doctor who lived across the road had been called, but he could do little for the wounded man. Inspector Walls died a few minutes later.

By this time another telephone call from the Countess to the police station at the town hall had resulted in the arrival of further policemen at the scene, and a search was made around the body by the light of bicycle lamps. A trilby hat was discovered. It didn't belong to any of the people clustered around the figure of the policeman, and the assumption was made that it must have been dropped by the fleeing assailant.

A few hundred yards away, near the top of South Cliff Avenue, a girl sat facing the sea – a very beautiful girl, and heavily pregnant. She gazed about her anxiously and, when she heard the sound of hurrying feet, turned her face towards the Grand Parade.

A young man panted up the steps from the Parade. He was hatless, and his rather long hair streamed out in the wind. He was a little older than the girl, probably in his early thirties, his rather prominent forehead giving him a studious look. He sat down beside her, gasping for breath. She grabbed his hand.

'Are you all right, John?' The boyfriend nodded. 'I thought I heard some shots?' John shook his head. 'Are you sure it was nothing to do with you?' She looked at him anxiously.

He took a deep breath and turned towards her, putting his arm about her shoulders. 'I can assure you, my dear Flossie, that it had nothing whatsoever to do with me. But if you think you can stand another little walk, perhaps we ought to be moving on. The night air is chilly.'

They walked to the Grand Parade and along the lower terrace which overlooked the beach, Florence stopping every so often to rest. Slowly they made their way back into town.

As they were going up Terminus Road, they saw a crowd of people outside the lighted window of a tobacconist – in those days it was the common practice to broadcast important news items by means of telegrams which were placed in shop windows. Florence pulled John over to the window and, looking over people's shoulders, saw the announcement that a popular member of the Parade police, Inspector Walls, had been shot down in South Cliff Avenue.

Florence dragged her boyfriend away from the window. 'John! I'm so frightened!'

He put his arm around her and kissed her on the cheek. 'Now, there's no need for you to worry your pretty little head.'

He smiled bravely, but in truth he was very worried indeed, for John Williams – or Scottie Shepherd, as he was also known – was a burglar and a jewel-thief. The son of a respected minister of the Church of Scotland, he had been in trouble with the police from an early age. After serving in the Boer War, he continued his life of crime and was deported from South Africa in 1907. Since then he had been convicted of a series of jewel-robberies along the South Coast.

'But you'll be bound to be suspected!'

'I know it, my dear. Especially as I'm in possession of a revolver.'

'John! You must get away!'

'I'll have to get in touch with my brother.'

'But he hates you. And so does that horrible wife of his.'

'No, he doesn't, my dear. And even if he did, he would help me, out of family honour.'

They continued their slow progress to their lodgings, and once there John wrote a hurried letter to his brother, who lived in London: 'If you will save my life, come here at once. Come to 4 Tideswell Road and ask for the name of Seymour. Bring some money with you. Urgent. Urgent.' They posted the letter soon after nine and retired to bed.

The next morning Florence went out to buy the morning papers. When she returned, she found John sitting on the bed with the revolver on his knees. She shuddered when she saw it.

'I wish you'd get rid of that horrible thing.'

After breakfast they took a stroll down to the beach, carrying the revolver, which was in two pieces, in a bag. At a point just below the Royal Parade grandstand, near the Redoubt, they sat on the shingle and tried to pretend they were just tourists enjoying a late seaside holiday. Then, under the cover of Florence's voluminous skirts, John dug a shallow hole and buried the pieces of the revolver.

John's brother, William, received the letter on the morning after it was posted and showed it to his wife and his friend Edgar Power, who had been a medical student and called himself Dr Power. His wife was against his doing anything about it, but Power was more conciliatory.

'He is, after all, your brother. The least you can do is to lend him some money. If you don't want to do it on your own, I'll come with you.'

'Don't be fooled by his charity,' said William's wife. 'He's more interested in that woman of John's. What's she calling herself these days? Florence Seymour? Getting herself pregnant by a man she's not married to! Little slut!'

William and Power caught the 1.27 p.m. train to Eastbourne, and William settled down to read the paper he had bought on the way to the station.

'My God! Have you seen this? A policeman shot in Eastbourne last night! I wonder if that's why John's in such a state.'

'Do you think he might have done it?'

William shrugged his shoulders. 'He's wild enough if he was cornered. And he does have a gun. Don't you remember? He came to see us last month at Digby Road and had a row with my wife and threatened her with a revolver.'

When they arrived at Eastbourne, William looked worried. 'I don't really know what to do,' he said as they were coming out of the station. 'If he's mixed up in a murder, I don't want to get involved.'

'I tell you what,' said Power. 'I'll go and see them, if you'll give me some money for them. Will you agree to let me see how things are and make what arrangements I can?'

'I'd be very grateful, Edgar.'

So William gave him two sovereigns, and Power went to Tideswell Road. He found John flushed and Florence looking tired and ill, lying on the bed.

'Have you brought any money?' asked John anxiously.

'All in good time.' Power sat down on the end of the bed. 'Have you anything to do with this shooting of the policeman?'

Out of the corner of his eye he saw Florence jump visibly.

'No, I haven't,' snapped John.

'Well, why the letter to William then, asking for money?'

'Because I've got to get away. Although I've nothing to do with this crime, the police know I'm in the area, and I'm the first person they're going to come looking for.'

'I think you're foolish to leave if you're innocent.'

'Listen, Dr Power. I know my business best. And if you haven't brought any money, I suggest you clear out.'

'All right, all right. Don't get hot under the collar. I have brought some money from your brother, but he's authorized me to do as I think fit. And I'm not going to give it you unless you agree to my conditions – that you go back to town with your brother, while I bring Florence later. If there is any trouble and you get stopped by the police, we don't want her involved.'

'No,' said the girl. 'I want to be with you, John, whatever happens.'

'I suppose Power's arrangement makes sense,' said John slowly. 'I don't want to risk your getting into trouble.'

After further protestations from Florence, this was finally decided. John and Power met William at the station. Both William and Power had bought return tickets from London, and Power gave his return half to John. When the two brothers reached London, they parted. John walked to Victoria to arrange accommodation for Florence at the Devon Hotel in Vauxhall Bridge Road. They had arranged to meet Power later, at Westminster Bridge Station.

After Edgar Power had seen John and his brother off on the train, he did not go straight back to Tideswell Road.

Instead he went to the police station at the town hall and asked to see the Chief Constable, saying that he had some information of the greatest importance to the murder investigation. As a result of this, when Power and Florence caught the London train later that evening, they were followed by two detectives.

Chief Inspector Elias Bower of Scotland Yard had gone down to Eastbourne early on the morning after the murder, with his assistant, Detective Sergeant Hayman, to take charge of the investigation. They were there all day and were present when Power had his interview with the Chief Constable.

The train arrived at Victoria at 10.23 that night, and Power and Florence were met by William, who took Florence to the Devon Hotel. John had been persuaded to keep out of the way, but the three men met later, as arranged, at Westminster Bridge Station and went to a nearby buffet for a drink.

Power asked John: 'Where are you going to stay in London?'

'I'm going to go to ground for a bit, see if I can raise some cash for a quick trip abroad.'

'Perhaps I can help,' said Power slowly. 'I know people who might be persuaded to lend you some. I'll see them tomorrow morning. Could you meet me at Moorgate Underground Station at, say, one o'clock in the afternoon?'

John agreed and the next day, a Friday, he was at the entrance to the underground station at the appointed time. He stood unobtrusively with his back against a wall and scanned the incoming passengers. Power was not among them. He waited for a quarter of an hour and was beginning to get impatient when suddenly three bulky men closed in on him.

'I am Chief Inspector Bowers from Scotland Yard. I am going to arrest you for murder at Eastbourne last Wednesday evening.'

John was driven to Cannon Row Police Station. He was kept there overnight and the next day, 12 October, taken by train to Eastbourne.

The news of his arrest soon leaked out and, when he arrived on Saturday afternoon, he was met by a large crowd. As he was being taken from the train to the town hall police station, his head was covered by a light cloth, to avoid his being seen by possible witnesses before the formal identification could take place. Since this was the first time this precaution had been taken, the case became known as 'The Hooded Man Case'.

Meanwhile Florence Seymour was in a state of terror. She had read in the papers on Saturday morning the news of John's arrest, and the same day detectives from Scotland Yard arrived at the Devon Hotel with warrants to search their luggage.

She didn't know whom to turn to for help, but on the Monday afternoon she received a visit from Power. His part in John's arrest had been kept secret by the police. She turned to him with relief.

'Oh, Dr Power, what am I going to do?'

'Well, do you need any money?'

'I haven't got much, but I don't want to take money from people.'

'I quite understand, Miss Seymour. I hope you won't think it presumptuous of me to say that I regard it as a duty to help anyone who is a friend of my friend John.' He took her small hand in his and, though she tried to withdraw it, pressed a sovereign into her palm. 'That should keep you going for a little while. Now,' he hurried on as Florence was about to protest, 'I understand that the police have been pestering you?'

The young girl nodded her head tearfully.

'I don't know if you will allow me to advise you. I can only say that I have had some experience of dealing with the police, and if you feel able to tell me what you did on the night of the murder, I might be able to suggest a course of action.'

Florence bit her lip. She didn't want to divulge anything of what had gone on between her and John. On the other hand, she desperately needed someone to advise her. She had no one else to turn to, and so far Power had been the only one to give any practical help.

Slowly she told him what had happened on that Wednesday night. When Power heard about the revolver, a gleam appeared in his eyes.

'Do you think you can remember where John buried it?'

'I don't know. Why?'

'Well, the most important advice I can give you is to move it. The beach will be the first place the police will look, and they'll soon find it, if it's not buried very deep in the shingle.'

Florence's face paled. 'Do you think so?'

'Certain of it. We must go down there tomorrow. We'll dig it up and dispose of it elsewhere.'

The next day they took a morning train to Eastbourne and had lunch at an hotel on the front. The young girl could eat little, but Power had a hearty meal. Then they went to the beach near the Redoubt.

'I think it was somewhere around here,' said Florence uncertainly. 'I'm very frightened that someone will see us.'

Power appeared to be looking around him and not at Florence at all. 'All right, we'll go back to the station.'

As they turned into the station entrance, the burly figure of Chief Inspector Bower appeared at their side.

They were taken to the police station. At first Florence denied all knowledge of a gun and that she and John had been anywhere near South Cliff Avenue on the night of the murder. But relentless questioning slowly wore her down. Most of the questioning appears to have taken place with the pregnant girl lying on a mattress on the floor of a cell, in a very distressed condition.

Power was allowed to see her. 'I think you ought to tell

the police everything you told me yesterday, and sign a statement to that effect.'

'But if I do, won't that go badly for John? Won't I in effect be putting a noose round his neck?'

'I don't see that you have any choice, Florence. If you don't do that, they will undoubtedly charge you with murder. And you don't want to go to the gallows yourself, do you?'

The girl shrieked with horror.

'I'm sorry, my dear. That was heartless of me. But I'm only thinking of your own welfare and that of the child – John's child, remember. You owe it to your unborn baby to protect yourself as much as you can.'

'I cannot betray John!'

But in the end the pressure from Power and the police was too much, and Florence signed a statement embodying the story she had told Power the day before. She was then released.

It was now nearly midnight, but the police, again assisted by Power, went straight to the beach. By the aid of lanterns they searched the shingle at the spot where Florence said she and John had buried the gun. An hour later Sergeant Hayman, sweating after his exertions with a spade, unearthed a piece of the revolver, and soon afterwards the other piece was recovered.

At last the police had enough evidence to go to trial. The felt hat, which the murderer had dropped at the scene of the crime, was discovered to have an unusual size, 7¼ – exactly the same size as that worn by John Williams, as the police proved by finding one of his hats in the luggage at the Devon Hotel.

Then there was the evidence of Florence Seymour, which put the prisoner near the scene of the crime at the right time. In addition, according to her statement, he was wearing a hat when he left her but not when he returned.

At the trial, which opened at Lewes Assizes on Thursday 12 December 1912, John Williams was defended by Patrick Hastings, destined to become a famous advocate but at that time only at the beginning of his career. He had a very difficult task for, although Florence Seymour repudiated her statement to the police, saying that it had been obtained by threats and coercion, it did little to benefit the prisoner.

According to his memoirs, Hastings was shocked by the horror of the case, by the treachery of Edgar Power and by the situation of a young girl having to undergo the ordeal of cross-examination in an advanced stage of pregnancy. She gave birth to a baby girl only a fortnight after the trial had ended.

Hastings' advocacy was not enough, and the jury soon brought in a verdict of 'guilty'. John Williams was sentenced to death. Hastings appealed, but the appeal was dismissed. An appeal for Florence to be allowed to marry John, to give legitimacy to the baby, was also turned down.

According to Hastings' memoirs, Florence was allowed to take the baby to see John Williams in prison, and the condemned man pressed a scrap of prison bread into the child's hand, with the words: 'Now nobody can say that your father has never given you anything.' The next day he was hanged.

4 Morris Clarke: Dry Rot

As Arthur Johnson drove his van up the gravel drive at the side of the farmhouse, he could hear his generator humming away to itself in its shed. He put his van in the garage and went in the back door of Crowtree Farm – his usual mode of entry. It was a Monday night, 15 October 1956, and Arthur had just come home after having a couple of drinks at the Greyhound Hotel in Peterborough, some seven miles away. He was middle-aged and lived alone on the farm, and it was generally believed locally that he kept large sums of money in the house.

Inside, he switched on the lights. Wearily stretching, since he'd had a hard day in the potato field, he realized he ought to go to bed but, still feeling thirsty, he went to a cupboard for a bottle of beer. He unscrewed the top, but it dropped on the floor. He bent down to pick it up.

That's when the lights went out.

Arthur cursed. The generator must have packed up again. Putting down his bottle, he felt his way to the back door. Outside, against the background of the dark sky, he thought he saw a shadowy figure.

'Hullo!' he called. 'Is somebody there?'

It was still dark, although faint streaks of light in the sky indicated the coming of dawn, when Lawrence Bell, a middle-aged farm-worker, crunched up the drive of Crowtree Farm. Normally the bulky figure of Arthur Johnson would come to meet him, but today there was no one. The farmhouse was in darkness, and the generator outside was silent.

As Lawrence passed the shed, he noticed a dark patch which, in the dim light, looked like oil against the light background of the gravel. He rounded the corner of the house and could just make out the dark bulk of the barn which was used as a garage. It was getting lighter by the minute, however, and he noticed that the doors were standing open and there was no van inside.

'Funny,' he muttered to himself. 'Arthur doesn't usually go out this early.'

Lawrence Bell had worked for the farmer for nearly ten years and knew the older man well. In fact, one of his sisters, Bessie, had been the farmer's last housekeeper.

He heard the sound of the other farmworkers coming up the drive.

'The old generator's been leaking again,' said one, noticing the dark patch by the shed.

'Somebody's been sloshing a lot of oil about,' said another. 'There's a big pool here.'

Lawrence stooped to examine a patch some twenty yards from the back door. He straightened, and his face was grim in the lightening gloom. 'Somebody better go for the police,' he said. 'That's not oil. It's blood!'

Chief Inspector T.O. Mills, of the Huntingdonshire Police, made a thorough examination of the farm and the farmhouse but failed to discover the missing farmer. He did discover large pools of blood on the gravel drive, and even traces of blood half a mile away, in a field which led to a canal, known as the North-Western Cut. But inside the farmhouse there was no blood, and no trace of a disturbance either.

There was no sign of a break-in. And it didn't look as if robbery was the motive for the attack. In a sitting-room on the ground floor, which testified to its little use by a strong smell of dry rot, there was a safe. A cloth covering the top of the safe had been turned back, but the door of the safe was still locked. A jacket hanging up behind the kitchen door had £10 in a pocket, and several other small sums of money were found around the house.

As the Chief Inspector was coming out of the farmhouse, he saw Inspector Carrington, who had been examining the fields.

'I think the attack took place outside,' remarked Mills. 'If you look carefully at the bloodstains near the generator shed, you'll see where the blood dripped when the attacked man was lying down. But there, over by that grass verge, you can see where the body has been dragged. I think he was felled by the shed. Then the assailant got out the van and loaded the body into the back of it. He drove across the fields, intending to dump the body in the cut.'

'Only he never made it,' replied Carrington. 'You can see the place out there on the fields where he turned round. There's a track which used to go all the way to the dyke. But this year the farmer set the field down to potatoes, and now it's crossed by big ridges. The van would have got bogged down if the driver had tried to cross. So he came back.'

'Hmm,' said the Chief Inspector thoughtfully. 'It seems like the man we're looking for is local. There was patchy fog around this area last night. Nobody but a local could have got a van up there, even halfway to the cut.' He paused. 'But there's one thing we must do before we do anything else. And that's find the van.'

They were lucky. The missing van turned up the same day. An employee of the London Brick Company, which had a factory at Norman Cross, some five miles to the south-east of Peterborough, was cycling home after a night shift. He saw a small grey van parked about thirty yards up a little-used lane called Two Pole Drove, some two miles from Crowtree Farm. Cycling past there later in the day, he noticed that the van was still there. He contacted the police.

The van was standing with two wheels on the grass verge. When the rear doors were opened, there was nothing but some old potato sacks inside. But they were saturated with blood. There was also blood on the inside of the van, and a big smear on the rear offside mudguard. It was plain that a heavy, bloodstained object had been dragged out of the van.

The next day, Wednesday, began with drizzling rain and, although it continued like that all day, a large force of police from all over Huntingdonshire combed the area around Crowtree Farm. In rubber boots they sloshed up and down the sodden fields and searched the ditches bordering them. The area around where the van had been found was also meticulously explored. But no further trace of the missing man was found.

At the end of the day the Chief Constable decided to ask for assistance from Scotland Yard. Detective Superintendent Wilfred Daws, affectionately known to his friends and colleagues as 'Flaps' because of his rather large ears, was detailed to go to the Fens. He took with him Detective Sergeant Humphreys.

Immediately, on Daws' suggestion, the search was widened. Frogmen were brought in from the Buckinghamshire Constabulary, and requests were made to all farmers to search their own fields thoroughly – and in particular to look carefully to see if their potato clamps, the long, triangular-shaped mounds in which potatoes were stored throughout the winter, had been interfered with.

Returning from a press conference at police headquarters, Daws turned into the doorway of the office which had been allotted to him. 'Care to come in for a chat?' he asked Chief Inspector Mills.

Mills nodded and followed Daws into the office,

followed by Sergeant Humphreys. The Superintendent turned to the Chief Inspector.

'What do you think happened that night?'

Mills scratched his chin. 'I think the murderer came by car.'

'Drove right up to the farm, you mean?'

'No, I think he stopped at Two Pole Drove, where Johnson's van was found, and left his own car there while he made his way across the fields on foot. I think he came to the farm secretly.'

'What for?'

The Chief Inspector again scratched his chin. 'The obvious purpose is robbery. He set out to burgle the farm, knowing that the old farmer had money concealed about the place, as most of them do around here. But the trouble is there's no sign of a break-in or the place being ransacked.'

'Have you looked in the safe?'

'We've searched for days now and haven't been able to find the key.'

'Have you tried the banks?' asked Daws. 'Sometimes people leave a spare key with their local bank manager.'

'I'll try that.'

'We'll assume for the present that the motive was robbery. If the man was local, he might have been known to Johnson. He could have knocked the farmer up, enticed him out of the farmhouse and killed him. If he knew Johnson, he might even have known where money was hidden, or he might have searched his victim and found his keys. That way he would be able to open the safe and drive away the van.'

'I think that's the most likely thing too. Having robbed the safe and killed Johnson, he gets out the farmer's van and bundles the body into the back. He dumps the body, drives back to his own car, exchanges vehicles and leaves the van behind him in Two Pole Drove.'

Daws nodded. 'It'll do for a working hypothesis. Now I

want you to continue to organize the search. Sergeant Humphreys and I will interview the locals, see if we can get a line on anyone who knew Johnson and might have wanted to rob him.'

Further information, which tended to confirm the robbery theory, came to light the next day. The manager of the Midland Bank in Peterborough reported that he held a duplicate key to Johnson's safe. He brought it to the farmhouse and opened the safe. It was empty except for some papers and an old handbag with a little money in it. The bank manager confirmed that Johnson had not paid a large sum of money into the bank recently, so it was very likely that the safe would have contained a considerable quantity of money.

As a result of questioning local people, on Tuesday 23 October, just a week after the murder, Daws, Humphreys and a woman police officer called at a house in Fulbridge Road, Peterborough. It was the home of Morris Clarke, his wife and six-year-old daughter. Clarke's wife, Eileen, known as 'Bessie', was Lawrence Bell's sister and had been Arthur Johnson's housekeeper. From 1952, when Clarke had finished his military service, till 1954 the whole family had lived with the farmer at Crowtree Farm.

Moreover, it was rumoured that Clarke had been heavily in debt.

At police headquarters in Peterborough, Clarke, a tall, slim young man with dark hair, explained how in 1954 his father and Arthur Johnson had loaned him some money to set up in the haulage business. He had continued with this until a few weeks previously, but by the sound of it had not been very successful. In a little under four years he had bought five lorries, most of them on hire-purchase, and sold all of them, the last one some two months earlier. He owed about £700 to Peterborough Engineering, a firm of motor engineers of Newark, and £400 to a Peterborough firm of lorry-distributors called Sellers & Batty.

Daws sat across from the young man in the interview

room. 'Did you give Sellers and Batty a cheque for £200,' he looked at his notes, 'dated 7 October this year, and was it sent back from the bank because there were insufficient funds to cover it?'

Clarke looked uncomfortable. 'That was an oversight on my part.'

'This was before the murder. And yet the day after the murder, on the Tuesday, you paid into the bank £200, enough to cover the cheque.'

'Yes, well, that was simply because Sellers and Batty were dunning me for the money. They sent a chap round to see me on the Monday night threatening court action. I hadn't realized that my account was that low. So I said: "All right. Present the cheque the next day and I'll see that there's enough money in to meet it". And I paid in £200 early the next day. It was a pure accident that it was the day after the murder.'

'Where did you get the £200 from?'

'I had it in the house. I'd saved it up.'

'Can your wife confirm this?'

For a moment the young man again looked uncomfortable. 'I shouldn't think so,' he said slowly. 'I don't tell my wife about all the money I have.'

'All right,' said Superintendent Daws. 'Tell me what you have been doing since you went out of business.'

Clarke explained that he had been working for Tower Hill Transport, a haulage firm in Peterborough. From six o'clock at night to six the next morning, his job was to ferry empty lorries which had been left by their long-distance drivers in a car-park in Peterborough to the brickworks at Norman Cross, some five miles away. There he assisted in loading the lorries with bricks and then returned them to the car-park in town, where they would be picked up by their regular drivers.

'Tell me what you did the night Mr Johnson disappeared.'

Morris Clarke ran a hand through his dark hair. 'Well, I

went on duty at six in the evening as usual. Normally, you see, I have four lorries to deal with each night, but that particular night only two came to Peterborough. At ten o'clock that night no more had arrived, so I phoned Charles Vaughan, the manager of Tower Hill Transport, and asked what he wanted me to do. He said I was to wait where I was. About 1.30 in the morning Albert Taylor came in with his lorry, and I hitched a lift to the brickworks.'

The Superintendent looked across at Clarke. 'What it amounts to then is this. You don't have an alibi between ten o'clock and half-past one? Nobody saw you then?'

'Yes, they did. As a matter of fact, I was seen by two police officers on the bridge near the centre of town about eleven o'clock. They asked me what I was doing, and I told them I was waiting for lorries to come. About an hour later I was talking to a blonde when a policeman came up and questioned me again. You can check all that.'

Daws arranged for a doctor to take a sample of Clarke's blood and then interviewed Clarke's wife, taking a statement from her. Then he accompanied the young man and his wife home and there took possession of some overalls, a blue wool blazer, a pullover and the grey flannel trousers which Clarke had been wearing under the overalls. All these, together with the bloodstained van and the sacks which had been found inside it, and samples of the bloodstains found at the farm on the gravel and in the fields, were examined by the staff at the Home Office Forensic Laboratory in Nottingham.

Two days later, on Thursday 25 October, a body was discovered, covered in sacking and caught in the weeds in a canal some three miles from Crowtree Farm. Superintendent Daws supervised the careful lifting of the body from the water and its laying out on the bank. The sacks were removed from the upper part, and it became obvious that the victim had received severe blows to the head. Lawrence Bell was able to identify the body as that of Arthur Johnson.

The body was removed to the Peterborough Memorial Hospital where a post-mortem was carried out by Dr David Fulton, the pathologist. He reported that there was no evidence that the man had drowned. Death was due to a series of savage blows to the head, some of which had probably been inflicted when the man was lying on the ground. Also, curiously, both bones in the right leg just above the ankle were broken. The extensive bruising accompanying the fracture showing that the injury must have been inflicted before death.

A picture was beginning to emerge for Daws of a brutal and probably unexpected attack on the farmer. Possibly laid low by a ferocious kick which smashed his right leg, he was then beaten about the head as he lay helpless on the ground.

Daws intensified the search for the murder weapon. Frogmen combed the canal near where the body had been found, and another search was made at the farm. All the buildings were gone through and heavy objects carefully scrutinized for bloodstains.

And after several days of drawing a blank, one morning Sergeant Humphreys rushed into his chief's office with the good news.

'I think we've found it! A piece of tree branch, like a large, round stick, about three feet long and quite thick, discovered under a pile of wood in one of the barns, and it looks very much as if it has bloodstains on it. And Clarke's alibi for the night in question is broken,' added the sergeant excitedly. 'You know he claimed that he was seen by the police on the night of the murder at eleven o'clock and again at twelve? I've checked with two PCs from the Peterborough Combined Force, and they did see him. PC Prior remembers it well, but it wasn't the Monday night, it was Thursday. It couldn't have been Monday because Prior was not on duty that night.'

Humphreys was plainly very excited about the prospect of success. Daws was more cautious. 'Don't forget we'll need the corroboration of forensic evidence to make this case stick,' he reminded his sergeant. How right he was to be cautious was shown during the following week.

Daws gave the news to a conference of the officers involved in the case. He tapped the papers in front of him on the desk. 'This is the report from Jack Fish, staff biologist at the Forensic Laboratory in Nottingham. First the good news. Reactions for human blood were obtained on the left leg of Clarke's trousers, on the front of his pullover, on the lapels of his blazer and on both sleeves. These, let me remind you, were the clothes he was wearing underneath his overalls on the night of the murder. Now the overalls themselves. You'll appreciate that these have probably been washed since the night of the murder, but there were several small bloodstains on the outside of the bib and the left leg.'

'Can I ask what the blood group is?' enquired Sergeant Humphreys.

'Group A,' replied Daws laconically.

'And Johnson's blood group?'

'The same.'

A sigh of satisfaction went round the audience.

But Daws began shaking his head. 'This is the bad news. Clarke's blood group is also A.'

'So Clarke has only to say that he's cut himself badly sometime in the past, and he can easily explain away those bloodstains on his clothes,' said Humphreys.

'True,' said Daws, 'but there is a bit more. Some scrapings from under Johnson's fingernails show blue wool fibres, which could have come from Clarke's blue blazer, and some blue cotton fibres, which could have come from his overalls.'

'Those overalls are very common,' said Mills. 'Almost everyone around here wears them.'

'I know,' replied Daws. 'It's all very slim evidence, as yet.'

He was forced to make the same point to his superior

officers, Assistant Commissioner of CID, New Scotland Yard, Sir Richard Jackson and Commander Hatherill, when he went to London to report later in the week.

But the Assistant Commissioner had more up his sleeve, and Superintendent Wilfred Daws stirred uneasily in his chair when Sir Richard produced a newspaper and tossed it across to him.

'Have you seen this, Wilfred?'

It was a copy of the Sunday newspaper *The People*, and in it there was an article by the nationally famous crime-reporter Duncan Webb, who had interviewed Clarke. The young man had protested his innocence, claiming that his alibi for the night of the murder was three police officers.

Daws explained that the alibi wouldn't hold water but had to admit: 'The situation is even worse than you think. Down in the Fens rumours are flying about thick and fast. Everybody knows we suspect Clarke, and the local newspaper also carried a report from Clarke where he says: "Do I look like a murderer?" and claims his name is being dragged through the mud.'

'It won't do, you know, Wilfred,' said the Assistant Commissioner sternly. 'It makes it look as if we're hounding the man. You'll have to do something, and quickly – the situation is getting out of hand.'

Superintendent Daws went back to Peterborough in a very worried state of mind. He was certain that Clarke was his man, but so far he had no proof that would stand up in court. He couldn't prove that Clarke had stolen money from Johnson, and he had very little evidence which would link the young man with the crime.

When Daws arrived in Peterborough, he went to a magistrate and asked for a warrant to search the Clarke house, in Fulbridge Road. Then he contacted Sergeant Humphreys. 'We'll try a last interrogation of Clarke, see if we can get him to confess. Then we'll search his house.'

But the long interview with Clarke produced no more

results. He repeated his story of what had happened that night and could not be shaken. On an impulse Daws consulted his notebook.

'We've got a statement from a lorry-driver employed by British Road Services. He said he gave you a lift from Bishops' Road car-park to the brickworks at Norman Cross at 1.30 in the morning. He also says you had a cycle with you when he picked you up in Peterborough and that he put it in the back of his lorry. Is that right?'

'If he says so, I suppose it must be.'

'What did you want the cycle for?'

'It's not mine; it's my wife's. Had a puncture which wanted repairing. I often have time to spare at nights, so I thought I'd mend the puncture while I waited.'

'You used that cycle to get from the Bishops' Road car-park to Two Pole Drove, didn't you?'

'No, I didn't.'

'I've had it checked out, and you could cycle there in twenty-three minutes. I think you left the car-park in Peterborough at ten o'clock, biked to Two Pole Drove, where you left the cycle, then walked the rest of the way to Crowtree Farm. When you got there, you switched off the generator outside the house to make Johnson come out, and when he did, you attacked him.'

'That's a lie.'

'I think that when he was unconscious you took his keys and robbed the safe, then loaded him into the back of his own van, dumped him in the canal and left the van in Two Pole Drove, and then cycled back to the car-park.'

'That's a load of rubbish.'

Daws said: 'I have a warrant here to search your house.'

'All right,' said Clarke with a smile, 'but I can't see what you expect to find. Even if you do find any money, you won't be able to prove it's not mine.'

Daws had a nasty feeling he was right, but at least he had to try. He and Sergeant Humphreys and some more police officers went with Clarke to Fulbridge Road.

They began at 2.30 p.m. and several hours later stood tired, dispirited and empty-handed in the small living-room on the ground floor.

'We seem to have drawn a blank,' muttered Daws.

'Wait a minute,' said Superintendent Beal of the Peterborough Combined Police Force, who had been helping in the search. 'As I remember it, these houses have a trapdoor leading up into the roof space. I think it's in the bathroom.'

'Let's look,' said the Scotland Yard man.

So up the narrow stairs trooped the party, led by Daws, with Clarke – and Sergeant Humphreys keeping a careful eye on him – bringing up the rear. They crowded into the small bathroom.

'We shall need some steps,' said Daws. A short while later, after mounting them, he pushed his head up through the trapdoor into the dusty confines of the roof space. He had brought a torch and shone it on the curtains of cobwebs and piles of dusty boxes that confronted him. But near to him were a biscuit tin and a bag. Both were nowhere near as dusty as the other objects in the roof space. He dragged them towards him and backed down the steps with his trophies in his arms.

Daws stole a look at Clarke, who was standing by the door. The young man's face was noticeably paler, but there was a look of determination on it.

The Superintendent wrenched the lid off the biscuit tin. Inside, packed tightly together, were bundles of pound notes from which rose a peculiar smell. Daws sniffed in perplexity. Then his face relaxed into a smile. He said to himself joyfully: 'Got you! Got you now, Morris Clarke!' but no words passed his lips.

Silently he passed the tin over to Humphreys. 'Smell anything?'

The Sergeant nodded his head, but his face wore a puzzled look. 'What is it?'

Daws answered, but his eyes were on Clarke as he did

so. 'It's dry rot! The same smell we noticed in the room where the safe was in Crowtree Farm.' He heard a gasp from Clarke. The Superintendent turned to the young killer. 'What's in this tin?'

The young man was shaking violently. 'It's Johnson's money.'

'Johnson, the dead farmer?'

'Yes,' he sobbed.

Clarke made a statement in which he admitted killing Johnson. At the subsequent trial, which was held at Huntingdon Assizes on 15 January 1957, before Mr Justice Donovan, the jury took just half an hour to bring in a verdict of 'guilty'. Clarke was sentenced to death by the judge.

Two days before he was due to be hanged, he was reprieved by the Home Secretary and the sentence changed to life imprisonment, which was usually what happened when a reprieve was granted.

5   John Gartside:
A Bit of a Wide Boy

'Come along. Don't walk in the middle of the road.' Mrs Buckley herded her two children back onto the grass verge, for, although it was 1947 and there was not the number of vehicles about there are today, this was the A62 road between Oldham and Huddersfield. Here it was almost a country road as it crossed the Pennines at the Standedge Pass, but on this warm afternoon in May there was still the occasional lorry toiling up the hill, on its way to the markets of Manchester.

In fact, it was quite a scenic route. The road looped round the end of a deep valley, which fell away to the right, and there was a scattering of houses high above the road, hugging the steep slopes of the wild and desolate Brun Moor, in the parish of Saddleworth.

But, as she walked along, Mrs Buckley was not thinking about scenery: she was wondering what was the matter with her friends the Bakers. She and her husband had known Percy and Alice Baker for a number of years but hadn't seen them for some time, so Mrs Buckley was walking the two miles from her home in the village of Dobcross to call on the Bakers at Standedge.

As Mrs Buckley and her children approached Manor

House Farm, the small, rather grandly named house where the Bakers lived, they were surprised to see a furniture van standing outside the front gate. It had the name 'Gold Lea & Co' on its sides. They came up to the garden gate just as two middle-aged men came out of the front door carrying a settee between them.

'Is Mrs Baker getting rid of some furniture?' asked Mrs Buckley.

The older of the two removal men lowered his end of the settee to the ground, wiped his brow with the back of his hand and shook his head.

'They're moving,' he said.

Mrs Buckley was astonished. 'They didn't say anything about it to us.'

The man shrugged his shoulders and bent to lift the end of the settee.

'But this is incredible! They've only been in the place since last September, and only a short time ago they were both telling us how much they liked living here.' Mrs Buckley stood aggressively in the gateway, blocking the path of the removal men.

The older of the two sighed and put his end down again; his assistant did the same.

'They've split up,' said the older man.

'Split up?' echoed Mrs Buckley in bewilderment.

'That's what he told me. Came into my shop last Thursday and said he and his wife had separated and he wanted to sell the furniture. He was going back into the RAF, so he said. He'd been in the RAF, I understand?'

Mrs Buckley nodded her head dumbly. Things were going too fast for her. The last time she'd seen the couple, they'd shown no sign of having disagreements. Now here they were apparently parting.

'I've got a signed agreement from Mr Baker, in my office, to sell this furniture,' said the removal man.

Mrs Buckley went home very puzzled indeed and immediately phoned her husband, who worked for the

National Coal Board. He was just as puzzled as she was.

'I think there's something funny going on,' he said. 'Did you get the man's name?'

'I got the name of the firm.'

'That'll do. I'll get in touch with Leonard Doughty. The Doughtys know the Bakers better than we do.'

The next day Ernest Buckley and Leonard Doughty went to the premises of Gold Lea & Co in Manchester Road, Oldham, and saw Philip Libman, the proprietor. He admitted that he had seen Mrs Buckley the previous day at Manor House Farm and showed the two friends the agreement form he had, signed P. Baker. Leonard Doughty took one look at it and said quietly: 'I've known Percy Baker for more than twenty years, and I can assure you that is not his signature.'

'Perhaps Mr Libman could describe the man who signed this form,' chimed in Ernest Buckley.

'Well,' said the proprietor, 'he was a young man in his twenties, with a bit of a limp. In fact, he showed me a scar he had on his left leg and told me he had been discharged from the RAF because of the leg injury.'

'That's not Percy Baker!' cut in Leonard Doughty. 'Percy's nearer our age, in his forties. And although he was in the RAF, there's nothing wrong with his left leg.'

'This is very serious,' said Mr Libman. 'There's someone going around impersonating your friend. And stealing his furniture.'

Leonard Doughty looked at Ernest Buckley. 'I don't like it one little bit, Ernest. As you know, we see the Bakers nearly every week – in fact, we have an arrangement that, if we don't arrive at their house by two o'clock on a Sunday, they come to us. But they didn't come last Sunday and I haven't seen them since a week last Thursday. They said nothing about going away and, as for splitting up, well, that's just ridiculous.'

Ernest Buckley nodded his head. 'Perhaps we ought to inform the police.'

A short while later Detective Constable E.W. Turner arrived at the premises. 'If you don't mind, gentlemen, I'll take statements from all three of you, starting with you Mr Libman.' He got out his notebook. 'Now, I understand that this gentleman calling himself Baker came to see you at this shop last Thursday. That would be 22 May?'

After relating the incidents of that day, including going to the farm with the young man, who opened the door with a key, Mr Libman reported that the stranger had asked £400 for the contents of the house. He called again at the shop in Oldham the next day, and they agreed a price of £300. He was calling himself Mr Baker at that time. They went again to the farm, this time to take a proper inventory of the contents.

'Did you notice anything odd while you were there?' asked the Detective Constable.

The proprietor scratched his head. 'There was one thing,' he said slowly. 'We were upstairs in a bedroom, and I noticed that there were some rings and a wristwatch in a bowl on a dressing-table. I asked him about them, because people don't usually leave things like that behind. He said one of the rings was his wife's wedding ring and she must have forgotten it.'

'Anything else?'

'There was another odd thing as well. All the time we were in the house, there was a dog barking in a shed outside. It went on and on so much that I eventually asked him why he didn't let it out. He said it would only run about and he would have to catch it again.'

The two friends looked at each other while Mr Libman continued with his statement.

'When the inventory was complete, I asked the young man to sign a form saying that he was the sole owner of the house contents. And this he did. I also asked for some proof of identity and, after searching for some time in a kitbag in the hall, he came up with an identity card in the name of P. Baker. I then gave him a deposit of £100.

Yesterday my assistant and I went to Manor House Farm to collect the furniture.'

'Can you describe the general layout of the place, Mr Libman?' asked the Detective Constable.

'Certainly. It's not a big house. There's a porch, and the front door leads into a large hall. This was used by the Bakers as a dining-room, for it had a table and four chairs, a sideboard and an armchair. It doesn't have a fireplace but the Bakers had installed an oil radiator. A door leads off into the lounge, which does have a fireplace and also fire-irons, two settees and two easy chairs. And then another door leads off the hall to the stairs and one to a pantry. Upstairs there's a bedroom, bathroom and toilet.'

'And you brought the furniture back here?'

'Yes, several loads.'

'And that was it, Mr Libman?'

'No, not quite. We promised that we'd drop off some personal property of this young man at a place in Uppermill.'

The policeman looked up. 'And where was it exactly in Uppermill?'

'I'm just trying to think. He told me the address, but I didn't write it down. I know it was a shop.'

'But you actually went there?'

'Oh yes. We took about ten suitcases and a linen box down there. And soon after we got to Uppermill, he rode up on a cycle and unlocked the shop so we could unload the suitcases. I gave him the balance of the money, which was £200. I also told him someone had been inquiring about Mrs Baker, though I didn't say if it was a man or woman. I asked him if he knew her address, but he was evasive. Then he said: "I'm not going to tell you, because this man you've been talking to is the cause of the separation".'

'Thank you, Mr Libman. We'll take you down to Uppermill later and see if you can identify the shop you went to.'

'Oh, there was one other thing. When my assistant was removing a carpet in the hall, he came across an empty cartridge. And we also found a rifle in a recess between there and the kitchen.'

After the constable had taken statements from the other two, they all went to Manor House Farm. But the place was locked up and they were unable to get in. On the way there, however, the two friends recognized Baker's car, a Morris 8, on the Uppermill to Standedge Road, but although they stopped and looked around it, they couldn't get in because it was also locked. There was no one nearby.

The police were eventually able to piece together the movements of the Bakers on that Tuesday in May. They had been away the weekend previously and had left their dog at kennels in Manchester. At about seven or 7.30 on the Tuesday evening, Mr Baker called to collect his dog. He was seen by one of the kennel staff, and this was the last sighting the police were able to obtain.

That same evening two more friends of the Bakers called to see them. They arrived at Manor House Farm at about 8.30 but found the place locked up. Looking through a window, they saw that a screen had been placed across the window so that only a small portion of the room could be seen.

But the strange thing was that Mr Baker's car was standing outside. It had the offside window open, and the driver's door was not properly shut. Not only that, but there was a suitcase behind the passenger seat. Plainly Mr Baker had left the car in a hurry, but neither he nor his wife nor the dog was anywhere to be seen.

Later PC Crooks from the Uppermill Police took Mr Libman down into the small mill town, and together they soon located the shop where the furniture-dealer had unloaded the suitcases.

'I think this place is rented by a certain John Gartside,' said the officer, who prided himself on knowing most of the shopkeepers in the town.

They drove back up the main street of the town in the police car and had gone only a few hundred yards when Mr Libman pointed out of the window. 'That's it!' he said excitedly. 'Outside the garage we've just passed. I'm sure that's Mr Baker's car.'

The PC quickly stopped and the two men retraced their steps. There was a car standing on the forecourt of the Central Garage. As they drew nearer, they could see that there was a young man bending down near the front of the car.

'I'm sure that's the man,' said Mr Libman, 'the one who sold me the Bakers' furniture.'

The young man was so occupied reading from what looked like the car handbook that he didn't notice the approach of the two men, and he started visibly when PC Crooks spoke to him.

'Excuse me, sir. Are you the owner of this vehicle?'

'Of course I am.'

'Will you tell me your name, sir?'

The young man suddenly noticed Mr Libman standing just behind the policeman. His face went pale, as he realized that the furniture man had probably recognized him, but he pulled himself together and decided to brazen it out. 'Certainly. My name is Percy Baker.'

'The person I saw had a scar on his left leg,' offered Mr Libman.

'That's me,' said the young man, and he pulled up the leg of his trousers so that they could see what looked like a wound scar on his left leg.

But the officer would have none of this. 'I know you,' he said. 'Your name is John Gartside.'

At the police station Gartside proved to have a very plausible manner. He maintained that he had bought the car from Baker for £200 the previous Friday and the furniture for £250 the previous Tuesday. Unfortunately he had no receipts for the transactions.

When asked why he had used someone else's name, he

said that he had used it at Mr Baker's own suggestion to speed up the deal with Mr Libman. He had been told that the couple were separating, but had no idea where they had gone. As for the rifle, he admitted that it was his but said that he'd left it for Baker to fix a faulty backsight.

Chief Detective Inspector C.D. Stubbs of the West Riding Constabulary was called in from Wakefield, and he held a conference of senior police officers in the station at Uppermill. Then he left instructions that Gartside should be held in the station while he went to Manor House Farm.

While he was there he was met by L.C. Nicholls, Director of the North-East Forensic Science Laboratory at Wakefield. The two men made a thorough search of the now largely empty house. While they were in the hall, the forensic scientist pointed out some marks on the walls and ceiling.

'Somebody's been trying to wash something off the wall.'

'Looks like blood to me.'

'Could well be. There's also some splashes up in the corner of the ceiling.'

Then they found what looked like bloodstains on a grating covering a drain. The scientist scraped some off, placed it in a container and took a sample from the drain itself.

The Detective Chief Inspector's face was grim when they had finished. 'It looks to me as if somebody's been killed here.'

While this was going on, Detective Sergeant A.E. Baugh went to Gartside's home. The young man lived at Laceby House, a two-storey building on the main Huddersfield to Oldham road. Manor House Farm stood above it, not 300 yards away, on the steep slope leading to Brun Moor, and from the front windows of Laceby House you could look across and see the Baker residence.

Sergeant Baugh made a painstaking search of the house

where Gartside lived with his father and mother, and found a blue suit which looked as if it might have bloodstains on it, though an attempt had been made to wash it. In a dressing-table cupboard in Gartside's bedroom he found a 0.38 Webley revolver in a leather case, and in a drawer of the same dressing-table a quantity of revolver and rifle ammunition.

Chief Inspector Stubbs began interviewing Gartside at 7.30 that evening, and the questioning continued until about 11.30, with the prisoner still sticking to his story. Then the detective was summoned to the phone. The call was from Mr Nicholls of the Forensic Science Laboratory.

'Chief Inspector? It looks as if you've got a murder on your hands. The blood is definitely human!'

The detective walked slowly back to where Gartside was being interviewed. 'We've now got evidence that someone might have been killed at Manor House Farm,' he told him.

'Who?'

'Possibly Mr or Mrs Baker.'

'What if it is both?'

Gartside then made another statement. In this he told how he had called to see Baker on the Tuesday night to discuss buying the car from him, and Baker had suggested he look at the bedroom suite with a view to buying that as well. According to Gartside, Mrs Baker had objected strongly to this, and an argument had broken out between them. Gartside thought they must have been arguing before he got there, for Baker made a remark about a boyfriend of Mrs Baker whom he claimed she had been seeing regularly.

While this was going on, he and Baker had brought down from upstairs a rifle and a revolver. They were going to try them outside later, and both guns were loaded and had been put on the settee. (They must have been in the lounge, as there wasn't a settee in any other room.)

Gartside then went on to describe how Mrs Baker

became angry with her husband and picked up a poker. Baker grabbed the revolver from the settee, there was a bang, and Mrs Baker dropped instantly. Gartside struggled with the man to try to get the gun away from him, and the revolver went off again. This time Baker collapsed, shot through the head. He was making a great deal of noise, moaning and groaning and writhing in agony. The young man didn't know what to do and panicked, picking up the rifle and firing two shots at the older man to put him out of his misery. There was blood all over the place.

Suddenly he heard a car drive up and two men got out, plainly coming to the farm. He hurriedly locked the doors and moved the bodies out of sight of the windows, pulling a screen across the main window to the lounge.

Gartside waited until dark, wondering what to do, then decided he must try to dispose of the bodies to make it look as if the Bakers had gone away. He dragged one of them up the lane, then brought the other across on a barrow and buried them both on the moor. Mopping up the bloodstains and clearing up as best as he could took the remainder of the night. He spent the rest of that day, Wednesday, wondering what to do and eventually decided to sell the furniture to make it look even more certain that they had gone away.

It was an incredible story but one which, given the self-confidence and plausibility of the young man, might just convince a jury that it was true. It was up to the police to subject the story to the most rigorous examination, point by point, either to confirm it or to prove it wrong.

They began at about five o'clock the next morning, just as dawn was breaking, when Gartside took the police officers up on to Brun Moor and showed them where he had buried the bodies. The grave was over half a mile from Manor House Farm and some 200 yards from the top of the Standedge cutting, through which ran the main road. It was in peaty soil and was only shallow but it contained the naked bodies of the Bakers, one on top of the other, together with a considerable quantity of bloodstained clothing.

Dr T.L. Sutherland, County Pathologist, made post-mortem examinations of the bodies. He reported that Mr Baker had three bullet wounds, two in the head and one in the body. One of the head wounds was caused by a 0.38 revolver bullet fired from close range, a matter of inches only. It had entered from the left temple and come out above the right ear. The other head wound was made by a rifle bullet, entering on top of the head and coming out just in front of the left cheek. The third bullet wound was in the chest, just below the ribs, and the bullet had come out at the back. The last two bullets had been fired from a distance of about a foot.

Mrs Baker had only one wound, caused by a revolver bullet, the scorch marks indicating a distance of no more than a few inches. It had been fired into her left temple, and this bullet was actually found in her head, so that the calibre could be confirmed.

The police, together with a team from the Forensic Science Laboratory in Wakefield, made a thorough examination of Manor House Farm. With the help of Mr Libman, all the furniture which had been removed from the house was replaced in, as far as could be discovered, the exact positions it had occupied when the Bakers lived there.

The trial of John Gartside opened on Monday 28 July 1947 at the Leeds Assizes, before Mr Justice Pritchard. G.H.B. Streatfield KC appeared for the prosecution, and the prisoner was defended by G.R. Hinchcliffe KC.

Streatfield was able to point out inconsistencies in Gartside's story. The police reconstruction, including the replacement of the furniture in Manor House Farm, had shown conclusively that there was no settee in the hall, on which, according to Gartside, he and Baker had put their guns.

There were bloodstains, however, on the walls and ceiling of the hall, and when the carpet had been removed, it could easily be seen where a bullet had chipped the floor. There was even a trace of metal left on the concrete. By careful examination of the mark, it was also possible to say from which direction the bullet had been fired and which direction it had taken after hitting the floor. There was no corresponding mark on the front door, which would have been in line with the trajectory of the bullet, so clearly the front door must have been open when the bullet was fired and hit the floor. Just as certainly the shooting had taken place in the hall.

The wound in Mr Baker's head was another inconsistency. According to Gartside, Baker was holding the revolver in the struggle. But Streatfield told the jury that Baker was right-handed, and it would have been physically impossible for him to have shot himself in the left temple so that the bullet travelled through his head and came out on the right side.

He suggested that Baker had rushed into the house through the hall door and that Gartside had fired at him with the rifle. The bullet had caught Baker in the stomach, had passed out and hit the floor. As the man was falling forward, Gartside had fired again, this time hitting him in the top of the head. And he had then finished him off with a revolver bullet in the side of the head.

The jury returned a verdict of 'guilty'. Gartside was sentenced to death and executed at Armley Prison in Leeds on Thursday 21 August, just three months after that tragic day in May.

But what actually happened in that small house high on the side of a steep hill on that warm evening?

The fact that Gartside lived only a few hundred yards from the Baker house and could see it quite easily from the front windows of his home must have had a profound influence on the tragic story.

Gartside had no convictions for violence. He might well have been a bit of a 'wide-boy', as petty criminals were called at the time, and have gone in for a small amount of stealing when he could get away with it. And he probably went to burgle Manor House Farm, having watched the Bakers leave by car and assumed they were going out for the evening.

As to why he took the guns is pure speculation, but he was in a rifle club, owned two weapons and was used to firing them – and it is well known that the possession of a gun is a boost to the ego of some young men. Whatever the reason for his having them, he must have picked them up when he heard the Bakers' car coming up the steep path from the main road.

When Mrs Baker stepped into the hall, she must have been confronted by Gartside, who held the revolver to her head. But somehow it didn't quite work out as it was supposed to. In all the Westerns and gangster films he'd seen, when someone produced a gun, he was immediately in control of the situation, and everyone went quiet and submissive, ready to do anything the man with the gun said. But Mrs Baker was terrified. She began screaming.

'Shut up!' hissed Gartside, holding the gun even closer to her head. 'Shut up or I'll shoot!'

But Mrs Baker was far gone in terror. She carried on screaming.

Gartside pulled the trigger. And that single action catapulted him from being a bit of a wide boy and apprentice burglar into a double murderer whose crimes shocked the nation.

6 Ethel Major:
Poison and Poison Pen

'Oh Lord!' muttered Sergeant Mitchell of the Lincolnshire Constabulary, 'Not Mrs Major again!'

He had just entered the little village of Kirkby on Bain, cycling down the long, straight road from Coningsby. The first houses in the village, on the left-hand side, were two pairs of semi-detached council houses, numbered 1 to 4 from the village end.

From number 2 there had issued the small, thin figure of a woman. She was in her forties and wearing a flowered apron. She had a long nose and spectacles, through which she gazed balefully at the policeman.

It was a warm afternoon in the spring of 1934, and the Sergeant had been hoping to meet one of his village constables for a nice chat on the prospects for the Heckington Agricultural Show or a discussion on whether Fred Perry would win Wimbledon again that year.

He stopped when he saw Mrs Major come out of her house and wondered for a moment if he could possibly pretend he hadn't seen her, turn round and cycle back the way he had come. But he knew that, if he did, she was quite likely to come shouting after him up the road, and the story of the burly police sergeant being pursued up the road by the angular figure of Mrs Major would be all over the village inside an hour. So he heaved an inward sigh and waited for the small woman to approach.

'Sergeant! I want a word with you about that good-for-nothing, drunken husband of mine! I've told you before and I'll tell you again, if you don't do something about him and that lorry of his, there'll be an accident and somebody will be killed, and it'll be all your fault, because you can't say you haven't been warned.'

'I know, I know,' said the harassed Sergeant. 'You've told me before about his being drunk in charge of his vehicle, and I can assure you my village constables have kept watch, but none of them has ever seen him the worse for drink when he's been with his lorry.'

'Well, all I can say is that you want to keep your eyes open then! Every night he goes down to the pub and comes home drunk as a lord. And then it's abusing me and his son.'

'Of course, if you suffer any violence, Mrs Major ... '

'Oh, I see. I've got to wait until I'm struck down before you'll do anything about it?'

The Sergeant eventually got away and pedalled off into the village with his ears burning and the back of his neck red. Of course, he knew all about the Major family. In these small villages, lying south-west of Lincoln in the shadow of the Wolds, everybody knew everybody else's business.

In some ways that was part of the trouble. Arthur Major had married Ethel Brown when he was on sick leave during the Great War in 1918. Arthur was eventually discharged in 1919, and they set up home with Ethel's parents. Unbeknown to him, she had borne an illegitimate daughter in 1915, when she was twenty-four. The girl, who was called Auriel Brown, was looked after by Ethel's parents and passed off as her sister, but you can't keep a secret like that for ever in small villages, and by the time that the couple had a home of their own in Kirkby on Bain, Arthur had learned of Ethel's guilty secret.

This was popularly regarded as the reason why the Majors rowed. Certainly it was well known that Arthur drank heavily, and the Sergeant was of the opinion that one night, when Arthur had had a skinful and come home in a particularly aggressive frame of mind, he might just lose control of himself – with disastrous consequences for all concerned. The Major family had the makings of a tragedy.

Sometime during the month of April 1934, Mrs Major received a poison-pen letter. It was addressed to 'Mrs Majar', and it read: 'You are sold now: don't you know how your husband spends his week-ends? He has got a nice bit of fluff now … You could get rid of him easy if you had him watched. Everyone knows about him and Mrs … ' On the back was written: 'I hear that he has now got a little "Majar" to look after.'

Mrs Major tackled her husband about it, but he denied that the accusation was true. She didn't believe him, however, and her suspicions received further con-firmation about a fortnight later when she intercepted a picture postcard addressed to him. It said: 'Dear A: Meet me same place same time: baby got prize.'

A bitter row erupted over the postcard and Major's infidelity, and the couple stopped sharing the same bedroom. Mrs Major still kept a close watch on her husband and one morning crept into his bedroom while he was still asleep and discovered an envelope lying on the floor. She took it downstairs and found that it contained two love-letters.

To my dearest sweetheart – In answer to your dear letter received this morning, thank you dearest …

Baroness looks as if she could kill me to-day (Wednesday). I am so afraid she should try to get Rita to go to her. I have told her if Mrs Major ever gives her any cakes or sweets she is not to go to her, she is to come running home.

I see her watching you in the garden and also Auriel but I do not care a fig for either of them …

Well now sweetheart, I will close with fondest love to my precious one.

From your loving sweetheart, Rose.

The second was quite as effusive as the first and confirmed Mrs Major's worst suspicions.

On Tuesday 1 May she went to see her regular GP Dr Armour. She threw the letters down on his desk.

'Now you can understand why I have been so ill of late.'

The doctor read the letters through carefully.

'Who do you think this "Rose" is?'

'Why, my next-door neighbour, Rose Kettleborough, that's who!'

Dr Armour nodded his head. He knew that the Kettleboroughs lived in the next pair of semis, at number 3 Council Houses, Kirkby on Bain. He tried to calm Mrs Major down, but she began a tirade against her husband, accusing him of many affairs with other women; her voice rising higher and higher by the minute, until they could hear her in the waiting-room outside the surgery. The doctor was glad when she went.

On the following Saturday night, when Major had presumably gone down to the pub or out with his lady-friend, Mrs Major called on Cyril Thornley, who lived in the same village. Cyril's father employed Arthur as a labourer in his gravel pits and also as a lorry-driver. She wanted to know how much Major had earned in the past week. Cyril told her that it was her husband's responsibility to tell her, not his.

This made her angry. 'People in Kirkby know that Major is idle and good for nothing. I'm surprised you employ such a man. You ought to sack him at once.'

It was round about this time that Major's drinking increased. Because of his drunken abuse on his return, Mrs Major and her son Lawrence, who was fifteen at the time, were forced to leave home at about ten o'clock each evening and spend the night with her father, Tom Brown, returning in the early hours of the morning. Brown was a retired gamekeeper and, since his wife had died, had lived with his granddaughter Auriel in a little cottage in Roughton, a village about half a mile up the road from Kirkby.

A week after Mrs Major's visit to the doctor, she rang the local council, with a view to getting a window repaired. John Holmes, Sanitary Inspector to the Horncastle District Council, eventually arrived at number 2 Council Houses.

'What's the trouble, Mrs Major?'

The opportunity was too good for her to miss. 'Drink, and my neighbour's wife, Rose Kettleborough, are the main troubles,' she replied tartly, and she promptly showed him the two love-letters.

Then she asked if she could be made the tenant of the house instead of her husband, but Holmes had to tell her that this couldn't be done without her husband's agreement. Mrs Major looked thoughtful.

Later that same week Joseph Kettleborough, from next door, was working in his back garden one evening when Mrs Major appeared. None of the four back gardens had fences between them, and so it was quite possible for her to walk straight over to talk to him.

'Mr Kettleborough, do you know that your wife has been writing love-letters to my husband?'

Kettleborough was considerably surprised. 'I don't believe it,' he snapped. 'Why don't you shut up and clear off?'

But Mrs Major was not put off as easily as that. 'You don't believe me? I always thought you were a good man.'

'Well, I'm not!' he retorted and carried on working. But if he thought that would shut her up, he was sadly mistaken. She carried on about the letters until in desperation he said: 'Well, let's see the damn letters, then!'

'I can't show them to you because a gentleman has them. But I warn you, I'm having this stopped.'

Soon after this the Chief Constable of Lincolnshire

received a letter from Kirkby. It was signed 'Parish Constables F.S. and C.D.', but the handwriting bore a remarkable resemblance to that of Mrs Major. In it the author accused Andrew Thornley, Arthur's employer, of using the gravel lorry illegally for passenger purposes and repeated the charges that Arthur Major was often drunk in charge of his lorry.

This idea of writing letters in other people's names seems to have taken a hold on Mrs Major's mind, for on 14 May she went to the offices of a solicitor in Horncastle, the local market town, and gave him the draft of a letter which she said was from her husband and was to be sent to Mrs Kettleborough: 'I request you to stop hiding any more letters for me and I shall not write to you any more and I don't wish to speak to you or have any more trouble with you in the future. Final notice.' She had put her husband's name at the bottom.

The next day John Holmes, the Sanitary Inspector, received a letter which was signed Arthur Major, giving up the tenancy of his council house. Holmes replied, accepting the notice and informing him that he would be the tenant until 11 June, when he would owe 16 shillings in rent.

It is difficult to see what Mrs Major hoped to gain by these manoeuvres, unless they were purely to annoy her husband. But if this was her object, she succeeded admirably – possibly too well, for it seemed to signal the impending break-up of the marriage. Major announced his intention of putting an advertisement in the local newspaper saying that henceforth he would not be responsible for his wife's expenditure. He had determined not to keep her any longer, for he began to buy his own food and keep it on a separate paper-covered shelf in the pantry.

On the Saturday before Whit Monday Arthur Major went into Horncastle. He visited first the offices of the *Horncastle News* to put in his announcement, then the offices of the solicitor to complain about the letter which had been sent to Mrs Kettleborough. He also called on Mr Holmes of the Horncastle Council, where he denied that he had written the letter attributed to him and demanded that the tenancy of the house be restored to him.

Sergeant Mitchell called at number 2 Council Houses, Kirkby, during the evening of that same Saturday, while Major was out. Mrs Major again repeated her old, familiar accusation that Arthur was always drunk in charge of his lorry. But this time she had something else on her mind. She told the Sergeant that she had been ill in bed about a fortnight previously and her husband had been in the habit of bringing her a cup of tea in the mornings, but she wouldn't drink it as he had put something in it to get rid of her.

Tuesday, following the Bank Holiday, saw Arthur Major back at work. According to Mrs Major, he arrived home that day at just after five o'clock and got his own tea. She was upstairs changing her blouse at the time but came down to find her husband sitting with his head in his hands.

'I do feel queer,' said Arthur.

Lawrence Major arrived home a little later and saw the remains of his father's meal on the kitchen table – corned beef, bread and butter, and tea.

A short while after this, Lawrence noticed his father mending a puncture on his bike in the back garden. He saw the older man fall down and rushed to help him, calling out: 'Mother! Dad is having a fit.'

Together they got the stricken man inside the house and sat him on a chair in the living-room. He was trembling violently.

'Do you think he's got a cold, Mother?'

'No, it's that corned beef he's always eating. It must have upset him.'

Arthur Major remained in that chair until ten o'clock at night. At intervals his legs jerked uncontrollably, he frothed at the mouth and he couldn't speak. It was obvious that, when these attacks occurred, he was in severe pain. When Tom Brown, Mrs Major's father, called later that night, he was astonished to see how ill Arthur was and surprised that a doctor had not been called. 'He said he didn't want one,' reported Mrs Major, but Tom Brown insisted, and in the meantime they managed to get the suffering man to bed.

Dr Frederick Smith saw Major at about 10.15 p.m. The patient was in bed and groaning in pain. His legs were jerking spasmodically and he appeared unable to speak. Mrs Major told him that her husband had suffered with fits for the past year or two.

Dr Smith instructed Mrs Major to give her husband nothing but fluids and a dose of castor oil when he regained consciousness, and he told her to send over for some medicine. He made up some opium solution when he got home, and Lawrence duly collected the medicine that same night.

The doctor called the next morning, and on the following day, Thursday 24 May, he found that Major was very much better. The muscular twitchings were now very slight. Arthur wanted to get up, but Dr Smith would not hear of it. He instructed Mrs Major to send over for some more medicine.

Sergeant Mitchell came in the afternoon and was told by Mrs Major that her husband was ill in bed.

'I'm sorry to hear that. What's the matter with him?'

'He has had fits. He will not get better and drive a motor lorry again.'

Some time during the evening Tom Brown arrived and found Arthur a lot better. A cup of water was fetched for the patient while he was there, but afterwards Brown could not remember whether it was Mrs Major or her son Lawrence who brought it. He left soon afterwards.

By ten o'clock that night, however, Arthur's condition had deteriorated alarmingly. Lawrence reported that his father had had another seizure and was foaming at the mouth. When that passed, the doomed man gasped: 'I am going to have another fit. I am going to die. Don't leave me yet.' But another spasm shook him and he expired.

The next day Mrs Major instructed her son to burn the paper from the pantry shelf on which Arthur Major had kept his food. She then told him to go into Horncastle and call at the offices of the *Horncastle News* and cancel the announcement which Arthur had placed several days earlier. She went to the doctor's and told him that her husband had died in the night, after another fit, and she wanted a death certificate.

'Why didn't you send for me?'

'We didn't have time, Doctor. It all happened so quickly.'

In view of Major's previous history of fits, according to Mrs Major, the doctor gave her a certificate stating that the cause of death was *'status epilepticus'*.

Mrs Major was in a hurry to get her husband buried. She had already suggested that the funeral should be on Saturday, but both Tom Brown and the undertaker said that was too early. The funeral was eventually arranged for Sunday.

But on the Saturday morning the postman delivered a letter to the home of the local coroner, who passed on the letter to the police. As a result, Sergeant Mitchell and Inspector Dodson called at number 1 Council Houses, to see Herbert Maltby, a disabled ex-serviceman. What he had to tell them cast new light on the death of Arthur Major, though his evidence was not brought to light until five months later at the trial.

The next day the Sergeant called at the Major house. He arrived at one o'clock and interrupted the preparations for the funeral. The guests were sitting round the little living-room.

'I'm afraid I must stop the funeral,' said the police officer.

'But I've got everything ready, and he's due to be buried at 3.30,' wailed Mrs Major.

'I can't help that. I've had my orders from the coroner.'

Later that same day Dr Armour and Dr Smith arrived with Sergeant Mitchell to perform an autopsy, which Dr Armour carried out, watched by the other two. He reported later that the body looked as if the man had died from asphyxia. He removed certain organs for analysis which were sealed in jars and handed to the police sergeant. They were then taken to St Mary's Hospital in London and given to Dr Roche Lynch, the Senior Official Analyst to the Home Office.

Inspector Dodson and Sergeant Mitchell interviewed Mrs Major, and she made the first of several statements. They also went to Primrose Cottage, home of Tom Brown, where Mrs Major and her son used to spend the night. Upstairs, in Tom's bedroom, was a chest he had had for many years. Being a retired gamekeeper, he was used to destroying vermin and occasionally putting down dogs, with poison. In a small compartment in the box was a bottle. The police sent it to Dr Roche Lynch for analysis.

Dr Lynch discovered that the bottle contained crystals of strychnine, a very violent poison. He also found that all the organs of Arthur Major he examined contained strychnine, in all a total of 1¼ grains. The analyst said at the trial that half a grain of strychnine had been known to be fatal, but his professional opinion was that between one and two grains would be a fatal dose for a man.

He also reported that the quantity in the stomach indicated that a recent dose of strychnine had been taken by the deceased. The first symptoms would occur from five to twenty minutes after ingestion: a tightness in the chest, restlessness, a feeling of suffocation and extreme anxiety. This would soon be followed by an extremely painful, uncontrollable jerking of the muscles, preceding generalized convulsions which would come on without any warning. The sufferer would eventually die from either asphyxia or exhaustion, and death would occur within three hours of taking a lethal dose.

Scotland Yard were called in, and Chief Inspector Young and Sergeant Salisbury arrived from London. They interviewed Mrs Major early in July and told her they suspected her husband had been poisoned. In answers to questions about where her father kept his poison, she said: 'He never talked to me about the poison he had in his possession. He's like me, keeps his affairs private. I know he kept a box by the window, but I didn't know what it contained. I have never had any strychnine poison.'

'I have never mentioned strychnine,' snapped Chief Inspector Young. 'How did you know your husband died from strychnine poisoning?'

'Oh, I'm sorry! I must have made a mistake.'

Put forward at the trial as evidence of her guilt, this statement was easily shown to be nothing of the kind. The strychnine bottle, labelled as such, had been removed from Tom Brown's box by the police on 6 June, and it had also been the topic of conversation between Mrs Major and her solicitor. By the time the interview with Inspector Young took place, nearly a month later, she had had ample time to have guessed that strychnine was being considered by the police in connection with Arthur Major's death.

A few days later Mrs Major was arrested and taken to Horncastle Police Station. The next day the police made a thorough search of number 2 Council Houses. They discovered a purse in which, together with several other items, was an old key. It was found to fit the poison chest in Tom Brown's bedroom. Told about this, Tom remembered that he had in fact lost a key to the box some ten years earlier, and he identified this as the one he had lost.

Ethel Major was brought to trial at Lincoln Assizes, held in the historic Lincoln Castle, on Monday 29 October 1934.

The judge was Mr Justice Charles. E. O'Sullivan KC led for the Crown, and Mrs Major was defended by Norman Birkett KC.

An important part of the prosecution's case was that Major had received two separate doses of strychnine, one on Tuesday and the other on Thursday night, and had died soon after the administration of the latter. With the known effects of the poison, submitted Mr O'Sullivan, nobody but a madman, having suffered the agonies of the first, would have given himself a second dose. Suicide was therefore ruled out, and having eliminated that, there was nobody with a better opportunity for giving the poison than Mrs Major. She had had access to the poison in her father's box by the key, and she had plenty of motive for wanting him out of the way.

Norman Birkett did his best against the overwhelming evidence, but the jury were absent for only a little over an hour before finding her guilty.

The judge, in sentencing her to death, said sternly, 'You have been found guilty of one of the cruellest crimes that you could have committed.'

Mrs Major was hanged at Hull Prison at 9 a.m. on Wednesday 19 December 1934. She became the first woman to be executed in Britain for eight years, and it created a national sensation.

Although convicted of what the judge described as one of the cruellest of crimes, Mrs Major had very nearly slipped through the net. If she had behaved in a reasonably sensible manner, shown a modicum of sorrow and regret for the passing of her husband and done nothing further to excite the suspicions of the already suspicious villagers, she might have got away with murder.

It was undoubtedly true that tongues would have been wagging from almost the beginning of this sorry saga, and the sudden death of Mr Major in such convenient circumstances would have been enough to raise the suspicions of the whole village, but there would have been very little to go on, and the police would have required some evidence for them to take action.

But two things went against her. One was the location in which the murder was committed and the other was a dog.

Next door to the Majors, at number 1, lived the Maltbys. Herbert Maltby kept two dogs. One was a brindle, the other black-and-white. Normally they slept in the house at night, but if the family went out in the evening, they would shut up the animals in the shed outside.

On Wednesday 23 May the morning after Arthur Major had first been taken ill, Mrs Elsie Roberts, from number 4, was attending to her poultry in the pen she had in the back garden. (She lived in the end one of the four council houses but, because the gardens had no fences between them, she could easily see across into Mrs Major's garden.) She saw one of Mr Maltby's dogs, the black and white one, come into Mrs Major's garden. Mrs Major came out of the house and scraped something off a plate onto the ground for the dog to eat. Then, after it had eaten, she laughed and went into the house. This was unusual to say the least, for she was known to dislike dogs in her garden. In fact, she had once thrown a bath at one to chase it away.

Later that same day Herbert Maltby locked his dogs up in the shed before he went out that evening. When he returned, at about 9.30 p.m., he found that the black-and-white dog was ill. Its joints were stiff, it could not open its mouth, and it appeared to be in great pain. He laid it gently on some sacks, but the next morning the dog was dead. He buried it in the garden.

This incident might not have occasioned any great interest in the normal course of events. Maltby's dogs were known to roam around the village and the surrounding fields, and it would not be all that unusual for a dog to eat some poisoned food which had been put down to kill vermin. But the coincidence of the dog dying so soon after being given food by Mrs Major, who was known to dislike dogs, was not lost on the villagers. And when Mr Major himself died, only a short time afterwards, the question was asked: 'Had Mrs Major done the same to her husband as she had obviously done to the dog?'

The letter which was delivered to the coroner on the Saturday and which sent the police to interview Herbert Maltby, recounted the story of the dog and its possible connection with the death of Arthur Major. It was signed 'Fairplay'. The authorship of the letter remains a mystery to this day, but it undoubtedly set the wheels of justice in motion, since the police exhumed the body of Maltby's dog, and it was found to contain strychnine.

7 Alfred Moore:
A Shot in the Dark

'Will he come, do you think?' asked Police Constable Arthur Jagger.

Detective Inspector Duncan Fraser nodded his head. 'We'll get him tonight.' He turned up the collar of his civilian raincoat and looked at the sky. It was a reasonably clear night, but there had been a forecast of rain later. 'Probably get soaked to the skin into the bargain, but we'll catch him, never fear. Better take up our positions.'

The two policemen placed themselves about eighty yards apart, astride a footpath which ran along the side of a field and up the hill to the farm near the top. Anyone coming up the path would easily be seen and intercepted.

They were part of a team of ten policemen from the West Riding of Yorkshire Constabulary, all in plain clothes and carrying whistles and staves. Their job was to surround the farm near the top of Cockley Hill, just outside the small mill town of Kirkheaton, on the outskirts of Huddersfield. It was about 11.45 on the night of Saturday 14 July 1951.

The occupier of Whinney Close Farm was thirty-six-year-old Alfred Moore, a poultry farmer who had lived there with his wife and four young children only since the previous May. A local man, he was suspected of being an active burglar. Moore had sent his two eldest children, both girls, to private schools, and was thought to have relieved the consequent strain on his financial resources by breaking into local mill offices and houses and stealing cash, postage stamps and valuables.

All this was only surmised by the police, for they had never been able to catch him – up till now. But tonight they knew he was out, and this time they were going to intercept him as he came back across the fields – they hoped – with the loot on him.

There was heavy rain later, but by the early hours it had stopped.

At just before two o'clock on the Sunday morning the stillness of the dark night was shattered by the sound of shots.

Police Constable W. Sellick, who was some hundred yards away from Inspector Fraser, heard five shots coming from that direction – two close together, followed by another three. He began running in the direction of the reports and, as he ran, heard the faint sound of a police whistle. He passed the place where the Inspector should have been, but there was no sign of him. He ran on. Approaching the footpath, he saw a faint gleam of light, which proved to be a torch lying on the ground.

Then he saw Inspector Fraser, lying motionless on his back. Nearby, a few feet further up the hill, lay PC Jagger. He was on his left side with his legs drawn up, in obvious pain from a gunshot wound in the abdomen.

After a quick look at the Inspector, PC Sellick bent over the Constable, who muttered some words in his ear. Sellick got to his feet and went a few yards up the path towards the farm, but he could see nothing, so he quickly returned to the injured men and summoned assistance by blowing his whistle and waving his torch.

Other officers were soon on the scene, including Detective Inspector Jenkins, who sent for ambulances. The injured men were carefully carried on stretchers to the bottom of the hill, where there was an old brickworks, and transferred to ambulances in the brickworks yard. At the hospital, Inspector Fraser was found to be dead. He had been shot three times from close range, once in the right wrist, once above the left elbow and once through the chest. The last one had penetrated the heart and killed him. PC Jagger had been shot only once, but that was in the lower abdomen and was a very serious wound. An emergency operation was performed immediately.

Soon after the shooting, the police officers remaining in the fields saw a light go on in the farmhouse. It remained on for about five minutes, then was extinguished. Detective Inspector Jenkins was in a quandary. It was a fair guess that whoever had shot his comrades had continued on up to the farm. Jenkins could rush the place, but the man was armed and none of his men was. He decided to send for armed reinforcements.

They duly arrived, led by Detective Chief Superintendent Metcalfe, who was in charge of the West Riding CID. At about four o'clock in the morning, some two hours after the shootings, he saw smoke issuing from one of the chimneys of the farmhouse. It didn't come out in a steady stream, however, but in a series of puffs, just as if somebody was putting things on the fire.

Metcalfe gave the order to close in as pale streaks of dawn were appearing in the sky. There were now a considerable number of policemen surrounding the farm, and one of them saw a shadowy figure at a downstairs window. He couldn't tell if it was a man or woman, but it was wearing a white garment like a nightshirt or nightdress. It appeared to stoop down near the window, then, as he watched, moved away into the room.

The Superintendent approached the farm. He was in plain clothes and unarmed, but he detailed an armed officer, PC Cleaver, to come with him. As they drew near the house, Cleaver saw someone move a curtain in an upper window. 'Up there,' he pointed.

They both looked up at the window and saw the face of

a woman. She was holding back the curtain and looking down at them. Just beyond her there appeared the face of a man.

'Come out!' called Metcalfe. 'We're police officers.'

The woman opened the window. 'What do you want?'

'We want to speak to Mr Moore.'

The woman was still holding the curtains. 'I'll come down,' she said.

Both the figures disappeared from the window.

'You stay a little behind me,' instructed the Chief Superintendent. 'But keep the gun handy just in case he's armed.'

There was short delay, then the woman opened a door. She was fully clothed, in a dress, hat and shoes. She looked very worried and upset. 'What do you want him for?'

Just behind her in the doorway could be seen the rather small, plump figure of Alfred Moore, with thinning brown hair, wearing a shirt and trousers and rubber boots.

Metcalfe advanced towards the man in the doorway. 'Come here!' he said.

Moore came forward reluctantly. 'What do you want with me?'

The Superintendent darted forward and grabbed Moore, and he was followed by PC Cleaver, who quickly put handcuffs on the farmer. He was cautioned by Metcalfe, who told him he was being arrested in connection with the shooting of two police officers.

'What did you do with the firearm?' queried the detective.

'Oh my God!' wailed Mrs Moore. 'There's a gun upstairs. I'll fetch it.'

She turned to go back into the house.

'Go with her, Cleaver.'

The PC accompanied Mrs Moore upstairs and came down carrying a shotgun.

Moore was taken to Huddersfield Police Station, where

he was questioned. He said: 'I went to bed with Mrs Moore and Pat' – his eldest daughter – 'at about twelve o'clock, or about a quarter of an hour either way. I never got up again that night.'

'In that case,' said Chief Superintendent Metcalfe, 'can you explain how your chimney came to be smoking at four o'clock this morning?'

'Well, if you must know, I got up to burn some rubbish.'

'What sort of rubbish?'

Moore hesitated. 'I'm not going to say any more about that.'

The Superintendent changed his line of attack. 'What firearms do you possess?'

Again Moore refused to answer any questions on the subject, saying he wanted a solicitor.

Up at Whinney Close Farm the police were conducting an exhaustive search of the buildings and the surrounding fields. Coachloads of police were brought in from other divisions to comb through the long grass in the field where the shooting had taken place.

Two police dogs were also used, and when the search by men and dogs had turned up nothing, a tractor was driven up to mow the long grass. Then the cut grass was turned over by rakes. The assistance of the Army was asked for, and a sergeant and five men from the Regiment of the Royal Engineers, stationed at Ripon, arrived with mine-detectors.

Eventually, near the place where the shooting had occurred, a bullet was discovered. It was a 9-mm round, and it matched the bullets taken from the shot policemen. It also explained why PC Sellick had heard five shots whereas the officers had only four bullet wounds – Jagger one and Fraser three. The Inspector had a large red bruise on his abdomen, and it was obvious that the gun had misfired and that the fifth shot had not had enough power to penetrate the skin. Since no ejected cartridges were found, it was assumed that the gun must have been a revolver and not the shotgun found at the farm.

Further discoveries gave ample evidence to suggest that Moore was a burglar. In a field near a beech tree a double-sided skeleton key was found, together with two other keys, some more keys on a ring and a jack knife. A live 9-mm round of the same type as the ones fired from the murderer's gun was discovered in the farmyard under some loose bricks, and in a tallboy in the bedroom there was a discharged 9-mm cartridge.

The police also solved the mystery of the crouching figure at the window. Below the window they located a hole leading to a cavity in the wall, and in this there was a veritable treasure-trove: gold and silver cigarette-cases, platinum rings and a gold watch. A total of 157 keys were recovered, which included safe keys and motor-car ignition keys, Yale keys and double-sided skeleton keys. In addition two more 9mm cartridge cases were uncovered.

Under a bed there was a pair of brown shoes which were still wet when found a few hours after the shooting. They had grass seeds sticking to them which were subsequently shown, by microscopic examination, to have come from the fields around the farm. A raincoat hanging in a wardrobe was later discovered to have a white hair on it similar to those of Inspector Fraser.

The fireplace still contained hot ashes when the police raked through it, and they found evidence that hundreds of postage stamps and some dollar bills had been burned there. A desperate attempt had obviously been made to get rid of incriminating evidence.

As the Sunday wore on and the police continued their painstaking search of the farm, at Huddersfield Royal Infirmary PC Jagger was fighting for his life. An emergency operation had been performed and he had received a blood transfusion, but the doctors were not optimistic. The wounded policeman might recover, but the odds were against him. The senior police officers realized that the constable's evidence would be vital. He was, after all, the only one who had actually seen the murderer and was still alive.

In the late afternoon Dr James Wrigley examined Jagger and gave his verdict. He was fit enough to give a statement and make an identification. The identification parade was held at the sick man's bedside.

Superintendent S. Foster, head of the Huddersfield Division of the West Riding Constabulary, assembled eight men, who wore raincoats like Moore, and he asked the prisoner where he would like to stand in the line. The poultry farmer chose the middle. The file of men were then led into PC Jagger's room, where they stood in front of his bed.

The pale-faced man in the hospital bed ran his eyes over each of the men in turn. Some were wearing suits under their raincoats; some, like Moore, wore sports jackets and flannels under the coat. Jagger's eyes came to rest on Moore, then passed on. He looked carefully at each man until he had reached the end of the line.

'Can you see the man who shot you in the line-up?' asked the Superintendent.

The wounded man nodded his head and pointed at Moore.

'Can you identify him,' persisted Foster, 'by counting from the left?'

Jagger did so, coming to rest on Moore.

'Now, can you do the same from the right?'

Again the PC finished up with Moore.

'Are you satisfied with the way the parade has been conducted?' the senior policeman asked Moore.

'Yes, but it wasn't me.'

A special court was convened, again at Jagger's bedside, before Percy Crowther, a local magistrate. The wounded policeman gave his evidence in a low voice.

He said that just before two o'clock he saw Moore coming up the path towards his home. Jagger approached. When the farmer heard the policeman's footsteps, he dived into the hedge. The PC shone his torch on him.

'I thought you were a cow,' mumbled Moore.

Jagger grabbed the man's left arm just as Inspector Fraser came up. He too shone his torch on the figure.

'Are you Alfred Moore?' asked the Inspector.

'Yes,' replied the poultry farmer.

'We are police officers, and you are coming with us.'

'No, sir! Oh, no, sir!'

Moore pulled a gun from his right-hand coat pocket and began firing. First he shot Jagger, who collapsed on the ground but was able to see what happened after that. Then he turned the gun on the Inspector. Fraser staggered away after being hit the first time, followed by Moore, who fired three more times, the last at point-blank range while the policeman was lying on the ground.

After Jagger had given his evidence, Moore was asked if he would like to put any questions to the PC, but all he could think of was to say: 'Are you quite sure it was me?'

'I'm quite sure,' came the reply from the man in the bed.

At 8.15 the next morning PC Jagger lost his fight for life. He was forty-two, a married man with two daughters. Inspector Fraser was forty-five and had been married with one daughter. Moore was charged that day with double murder.

The search went on at the farm for several weeks. Feeding-troughs and ponds were emptied, piles of farm machinery and accumulated rubbish were moved. Walls were knocked down, and where this was not possible, the crevices between the bricks were examined minutely to see if any bricks had recently been removed or anything pushed in between. The farmhouse itself was practically taken apart brick by brick. But the gun which killed the policemen was not found. And neither was any loot discovered which could be attributed to a robbery done that night.

The police also questioned Moore's brother, Charles. He was a textile worker and lived only a mile and a half from

Whinney Close Farm. He had been at the farm that Saturday, since midday, helping his brother build a pigsty, and had stayed rather later in the evening than he had intended and missed the last bus home. When he decided to walk home across the fields, Alfred said he would go with him. They set out at just after 11 p.m. and walked down through the fields following the same footpath which was to be the scene of the tragedy a few hours later. They stopped at the junction of Waterloo Rise and Fleminghouse Lane. Charles asked his brother if he wanted to come home with him for a cup of tea, but Alfred declined.

'I won't bother, thanks. I've promised to get back.'

'Will you go back the same way?'

'No, it's bad luck to turn back. I'll go round by Fleminghouse Lane.'

They parted at about 11.20 p.m. and Charles reached home at 11.35 p.m. The police retraced Alfred Moore's steps and claimed that he could not have reached his home in less than thirty minutes, which would make it about 11.50 p.m. Since they had set their cordon by 11.45, they believed he could not have got home without having had to pass through the cordon first.

Alfred Moore went to trial on Monday 10 December 1951, at Leeds Assizes, before Mr Justice Pearson, with G. Raymond Hinchcliffe KC prosecuting and H.B.H. Hylton-Foster KC leading for the defence.

The prosecution case rested on the premise that Moore could not have passed through the police cordon if he had arrived earlier and therefore it must have been he who came up the hill at 1.55 on that Sunday morning and shot the two police officers. He was also seen by PC Jagger, who then picked him out at an identification parade.

Empty cartridges of the type which had been used to kill the officers had been found at the farm, together with ample evidence that he had been carrying on a burglary business for some time.

Although the gun was never recovered, the police had found Joe Baxter, a driver employed by a firm of removal contractors, who had helped the Moores move to Whinney Close Farm, the previous May, and who recalled an incident when he and Alfred Moore were lifting a black tool box into the removals lorry. The box had burst open and inside Baxter was able to see, among the rusty nails, saw blades and small tools, what appeared to be a German Luger revolver. He had received small arms training in the Royal Navy and claimed to know the difference between a revolver and an automatic pistol. The revolver he saw appeared to be in a dilapidated and rusty condition.

In the opinion of Dr Horace Mays, of the Home Office Section of the Ministry of Supply, Woolwich Arsenal, all the bullets taken from the shot policemen and the cartridges collected by the police could have been fired from the same gun.

There was also the wet pair of brown shoes found underneath the bed in Whinney Close Farm which had grass seeds and loam soil adhering to them and which had presumably been worn outside not very long before they were found. Then there was the raincoat with the white hair on it which could have come from the head of Inspector Fraser.

Counsel for the defence pointed out that 9-mm ammunition was one of the most common calibres and that the cartridges obtained at the farm were of varied dates of manufacture. And he was able to get Dr Mays to admit that the striker marks on the cartridges showed they could not have been fired from a Luger. He also argued that, from the number of people who had handled the raincoat, the presence of one white hair was not conclusive evidence that it had been in contact with Inspector Fraser.

The jury of ten men and two women took under an hour to bring in a verdict of 'guilty'. Mr Justice Pearson, whose first murder trial this was after his being appointed a judge, was visibly moved as he sentenced Moore to death.

Mr Hylton-Foster appealed against the verdict, but the appeal was rejected on Monday 21 January 1952. Moore's solicitor petitioned the Home Secretary for a reprieve, but it was refused and Moore was hanged at Armley Gaol, Leeds, on Wednesday 6 February 1952.

Was Moore really guilty? Or was an innocent man hanged?

The police reported that their cordon was set by 11.45 p.m. or a little before. Moore could have reached home by 11.50 p.m. A few minutes either way in the time-estimates could have meant that Moore might have gone through before the cordon was quite set.

Mr Hylton-Foster, in his speech for the defence, showed why the location of this crime had had such an important effect on it. He pointed out that the police had gone to their respective positions from the brickworks, which is at the bottom of the hill, almost due south of Whinney Close Farm. Moore would be coming up a path further to the west, and it may well have been that the routes, of the police on the one hand and Moore on the other, did not overlap. Being a small man, he would not easily be seen against the background of the hedges and the long grass. And while the officers were taking up their positions, they would not be expecting anything to happen straight away.

Far from the police officers being able to spot Moore, since he was coming up the hill at an angle to their route from the brickworks, he might well have been able to see them. The hill on which the police were posted is largely treeless, with only hedges to break the skyline. A body of men moving up the hill would be easier to see than a single dumpy figure.

Mr Hylton-Foster surely had a strong point when he said that, with such a narrow margin of timing between the arrival of the officers and Moore's leaving his brother, he could not be satisfied that the police could be certain that no one had passed them.

The crucial part of the case against Moore was the evidence of PC Jagger, who had clearly identified the poultry farmer as being the man he saw in the field. But a most serious omission, as Fenton Bresler has pointed out in his book *Scales of Justice,* as far as Moore was concerned, was that at the court convened at the dying man's bedside he was not represented by a lawyer. It was nobody's fault. It was a Sunday, and the solicitor Moore had asked for simply could not be found. The police could not wait, as there was no telling how long PC Jagger would last. But the fact remains that the accused man did not have the assistance of a solicitor, who might have questioned, for example, how certain the PC could be of identification when he saw the man only in the dark, by torchlight? Jagger had had at most a fleeting glimpse of the murderer, and the light of a torch can easily distort features, particularly when it is held to one side.

And so the evidence of the officer went virtually unchallenged, which, as far as Moore was concerned, cost him his life.

8   Albert Burrows:
One Thing Leads to Another

'Why don't we go out for a drink?' The big man turned to the small figure of the woman.

'But it's Sunday.'

'Well, we're not thinking of going to church, are we?' He laughed derisively.

'There's no need to laugh in that coarse way. I don't think it's right to go out drinking on a Sunday,' said the woman rather primly. In 1920 people took Sunday observance a lot more seriously than they do today.

'If you're not coming, I'm going on my own!' She could hear the familiar temper rising in his voice. 'I need something to take my mind off things.'

She nodded her head quickly to placate him. She knew that he was out of work and owed several months rent on the house. And then there was the court case coming up the next day.

She didn't want to go but, if there were any women at any of the pubs he was likely to visit, well…. Although he was nearly thirty years older than she was, she still didn't trust him not to pick up some other young girl and be gone from her life.

'What about the children?'

'We can leave little Elsie for an hour, can't we? And you can take the baby with you. There's a nice pub up on the moors, the Hare and Hounds. They won't mind if you take the baby in the bar.'

'Are you sure? It's illegal, you know.'

'The landlord's a friend of mine, and at this time of night' – they could hear the church bells tolling, so it must be about six – 'there won't be many people in.'

A few minutes later, on that dark Sunday night in January, the couple left their little house in Glossop and set off across the moors, the woman carrying the baby in her arms.

Nobody saw the woman or the baby alive again.

On 4 March, another Sunday, three years later, in 1923, in the same small Derbyshire town set in the foothills of the Pennines, a three-year-old boy called Tommy Wood was playing at his uncle's fishmonger's shop just round the corner from where he lived. At about eleven o'clock in the morning the fishmonger told him to go to his grandfather's house, a few streets away. This was the normal practice, as the boy usually had his Sunday dinner with his grandparents.

When young Tommy had not come back home by tea-time, his mother called at the grandparents' house, expecting the boy to be there, but they hadn't seen him all day.

Father and mother, together with numerous relatives, then began a search of all the streets in the area. They questioned other children, who knew little Tommy, but nobody had seen him since before midday.

The distraught parents went to the police, who quickly mobilized a search of the town – in particular near a stream which originates in the hills above the town and runs by Slatelands Road, close to where little Tommy had been reported seen. With the recent heavy rain, the normally placid stream was now a raging torrent – a boy of ten had once been swept to his death at the same spot.

The search continued until dark and then was abandoned until the next morning. At first light a large contingent of police and voluntary helpers began to search outhouses and sheds, back gardens, mills and factory buildings which had been left empty over the weekend. They had no success.

The search then spread to the hills, valleys and streams which surround the small town. By this time the number of people involved ran into hundreds. A bloodhound was brought in, and the animal searched up and down the stream which runs by Slatelands Road, and the watercourse was dragged by the police up and down its length. But they found no trace of the little boy.

The police questioned a large number of people in the area where Tommy lived but could find no one who had seen him after eleven o'clock. But on the Monday, the day after the boy disappeared, a man handed in a written statement at the police station saying that he had seen him at 1.30 p.m. playing with some other boys near the stream.

The same day the man went to the boy's home. Finding only the grandmother there, he repeated what he had said in his statement. He also remarked that he'd heard the little boy say that other boys had thrown his purse into a hen pen, and he offered to show her where it was. She collected some more women to go with her, and together they went to the place the man pointed out. Sure enough, there was Tommy's purse in the hen pen.

Inspector J. Chadwick, of the Glossop Borough Police, who was in charge of the case, then interviewed him. The man, whose name was Albert Edward Burrows, was in his sixties and lived across the road from little Tommy. Burrows said that on Sunday morning he had left home at about 11.30 to go across the moors to Hargate Hill, near a village called Simmondley, to look for a farmer about carting some manure. He couldn't find the farm, however, and returned to Glossop via Slatelands Road, where he had seen young Tommy by the stream. He also said he had seen a number of people on his walk, including a friend called Shortland who had also seen the boy.

During the following week the police and their helpers, who included Burrows, continued their search of the surrounding moors, and the police also continued to interview people.

On Monday 12 March, over a week after the disappearance of the little boy, the Inspector again talked to Burrows at the police station.

'Mr Burrows,' he said, 'you've made a number of statements to the police, and I don't think any of them are quite true. You say you didn't see the child until 1.30, and yet we have a witness who saw you in Slatelands Road between eleven and 11.30, with a young child, who he thinks was a boy, and he saw you give this boy an apple.' Burrows said nothing. 'Then we've found a young lad who was leading a horse in Slatelands Road at about the same time, and he saw you, with a child, going towards the open country.'

'I don't know any young lads like that.'

'He knows you by name, anyway. There's also a young lady who was out walking on Sunday morning. She went through Simmondley and saw a man and a boy climbing on the shale some distance away on her left. That would be about twelve o'clock.'

'I suppose she recognized me as well?'

'No, the man was too far away for that.'

'Well, it certainly wasn't me!'

'Perhaps you remember talking to a man on Hargate Hill near the entrance to the stone quarry, about half-past twelve?'

'I remember that.'

'And you had no child with you then?'

'Of course I didn't. I never saw that child until 1.30. And Tom Shortland can prove it.'

'We've talked to Mr Shortland. Though he did see some

children in Slatelands Road at 1.30, none of them was as young as four years, and we have the witnesses who saw you with the child earlier. We'll find that child eventually, Mr Burrows, with your help or not. We'll search all over those moors until we do. Mr Burgess, the man you talked to by the stone quarry, said there are some air shafts up there.'

Burrows' face went white, and he moistened his dry lips with his tongue.

'All right,' he said after a long pause. 'I did lie. I did see the boy. I live just across the street from him, and he's always pestering me to take him for walks. I did so that Sunday. I took him up on the moors. He wanted me to catch him a rabbit. So I left him in a hollow while I went to set some snares. I was only gone about ten minutes, but when I got back he had disappeared. I was very upset and searched for a long time. But eventually I had to come back.'

'Would you show us where you left the boy?'

Burrows took Inspector Chadwick, Sergeant Wilson and the Chief Constable of the Glossop Borough Police up Hargate Hill to the place where he said he had left little Tommy Wood. There were gorse bushes all around, and nearby a deep pond. And about 200 yards away there was top of an air shaft.

In the 1920s these air shafts dotted the area, mute reminders of the coal-mining which had taken place beneath the hills in the last century, until the seams gave out. They were mostly disused, each one a hundred or more feet deep, six feet across and usually with water in the bottom. They were often used by farmers for getting rid of rubbish or dead animals.

After a careful search of the ground and the pond, the Chief Constable decided they should look at the air shaft. Grappling-hooks were fetched and lowered down the shaft, which had only a wooden fence around it, the opening was almost overgrown with bushes. They worked until nightfall but found no trace of the child.

The next day, this time without Burrows, the police went further down the hill to another air shaft from the old Dinting Colliery. This lay on the other side of the Glossop road and had a crumbling six-foot wall around it, across which the police placed planks. PC Roe sat perilously on one of the planks, above the hundred-foot drop, and lowered his rope with the grappling-irons on it. He felt a weight and began hauling up, but all they had secured was a basket filled with stones and tin cans. He lowered again.

After several more unsuccessful attempts Roe again felt a resistance and began pulling up. When the object reached the light, the watchers could see that a body was caught on the hooks.

They had found little Tommy Wood.

The Chief Constable, who had been watching the operations, had noticed a figure spying on them from the top of the hill, and he guessed that this was Burrows. As soon as the body was brought up, he gave orders that the hill should be surrounded by the police. But a motley crowd of civilians was also watching the operations, including young Tommy's uncle, who identified the body, and they decided to take matters into their own hands. They quickly pursued Burrows and caught him where he was hiding under a holly bush.

He was roughly handled by the crowd of men and cried for mercy.

'You didn't show much mercy to little Tommy,' said one of them.

'I don't know what made me do it,' muttered Burrows.

The crowd began to utter threats against the prisoner.

'Don't touch my wife, will you?' he pleaded. 'She's innocent.'

Sergeant Wilson arrived eventually, and the men reluctantly handed over the frightened man to the police officer.

'He said he had a brother in the asylum,' jeered one.

Burrows seemed to recover some of his composure when he was in the hands of the police officer. To the cat-calling crowd which followed him down the road he turned and boasted: 'I shan't tremble on the scaffold.'

He was taken to the police station, while the body of the little boy was removed to the mortuary.

The post-mortem, which was carried out by Dr James Henry Dible, Lecturer in Bacteriology at the University of Manchester, and Dr Milligan, revealed that the child had died a horrible death. The presence of water in the lungs showed that he had died from drowning at the bottom of the pit, which was found to be 105 feet deep and which was filled with filthy water to a depth of eight feet.

And there was clear evidence that he had been the victim of a savage sexual assault before being hurled into the shaft.

'This man's a monster,' said the Chief Constable, when he heard the news.

'I have a feeling,' said Inspector Chadwick slowly, 'that he's even worse than we think.' They were sitting together in the Chief Constable's office. 'I've come across him before,' continued the Inspector, rubbing a hand across his chin. 'And considering that he's in his sixties, he seems to have a remarkable sexual appetite.'

'A disgusting and unnatural one, by the sound of it.'

'That may well be, sir, but three or four years ago I had occasion to arrest him for non-payment of a bastardy order which a woman in Nantwich had obtained against him.'

'Well, that's not a hanging crime is it?'

'No, sir, but if you'll just let me continue. He was already married. Been married to his present wife for some twenty years, I understand. But during the war he went to work in a munitions factory and took up with this woman, by name Hannah Calladine. She had a child by him in 1918, and in the same year he bigamously married her. It was quickly discovered, however, and he got six months.'

'Yes, I remember the case.'

'Yes, sir. Well, when he came out, he seems to have gone

back to his wife, but this Hannah Calladine, who already had another illegitimate child, a four-year-old girl, at once applied for a bastardy order against him. He never paid a penny towards it, and in November 1919 I arrested him and he was gaoled for twenty-one days.'

'I'm sure this is all very interesting,' said the Chief Constable, 'but what's it got to do with the present case?'

'I'm coming to that, sir,' said the Inspector in an aggrieved tone. 'You see, in December of that same year, when Burrows was living with his wife in Back Kershaw Street, Hannah Calladine arrives on his doorstep, together with the two children!'

The Inspector's superior allowed himself a slight smile. 'Serves him right, I would say.'

'Oh yes, I agree with you, sir. But his wife didn't see it like that. Burrows took Hannah in, saying he couldn't send her back to Nantwich on a night like that, but the very next day his wife upped and left him. And then she applied for a maintenance order herself under the Married Women's Act.'

'Oh yes, I remember. It was in all the newspapers. "Glossop man's two wives, both in the house at the same time". Created a sensation in the town.'

'Yes, that's right, sir. She got an order against him for £1 a week. But the thing was that she went back to him only a week later, because Hannah Calladine had disappeared quite suddenly. And she's never been seen in Glossop since. There's been talk down in that part of the town for years about what happened to the girl and her children. Burrows always tells people that she's working in Manchester.'

'And you think he's done away with them too?'

'All I'm saying, sir, is that we ought to have another look at that air shaft at the Dinting Colliery.'

'Now, just you hold your horses, Inspector! We don't want to go off at half cock. This woman and her family may simply be living quietly somewhere. We must first check with any relatives and see if they've heard from her. Then we must advertise in the press and ask for any information about her. But just the same,' the Chief Constable tapped his fingers on the desk in front of him, 'I think I'll get in touch with the colliery people and make inquiries about draining that shaft.'

The police located a sister of the missing woman, a Miss Mary Elizabeth Calladine, who lived with her aged parents in a small cottage near Nantwich. She reported that they had received many letters and postcards from Burrows since her sister had left home in December 1919 to join him in Glossop, but none from the girl herself. As recently as 9 January 1923 they had received a letter from Burrows asking them to send the birth certificates of the two children, as he had put them in a burial club at a penny a week and the organizer had asked for proof of the children's ages. Both children, reported Burrows, were in Chinley Hospital with diphtheria.

Further police operations on the Dinting Colliery air shaft were begun on 7 May. It was bitterly cold up on the Derbyshire hills, and there had been heavy falls of snow. The policemen were lowered down the shaft in a wooden box suspended by a rope secured to a derrick erected over the shaft and operated by a winch. To protect the men at the top, Inspector Chadwick had arranged for a tarpaulin-covered shed to be built, and a pump was used to remove water from the shaft.

The presence of rotting animal carcases in the bottom of the shaft, stones which had fallen from the walls, tin cans and hardware of all kinds and, of course, the putrid water made working conditions very difficult.

Soon after the beginning of operations, Mr Greenwood, a local colliery owner, and PC Roe were descending in the box when the derrick collapsed, nearly throwing them out, upsetting their lamp and leaving them suspended in darkness half way down the shaft. It was only with great difficulty that they were hauled up by hand.

With the assistance of the Glossop Fire Brigade's pumping equipment, much of the water and some of the refuse had been removed from the shaft by the evening of Saturday the 19th. It had been hoped to carry on operations far into the night, but the men were too exhausted to continue, and the Chief Constable called a halt. Heavy rain fell that night, and by the morning, when the men returned, water gushing through the loosely jointed stones of the walls had refilled the shaft to the old level.

The Bank Holiday arrived, together with huge crowds from Manchester and the surrounding district who lined the roads and dotted the fields around the site. Rather nearer, under a tarpaulin, an army of pressmen and photographers waited patiently for something sensational to happen.

By Wednesday 23 May several tons of debris had been removed from the now comparatively dry shaft. Then PC Roe and James Hilton, a colliery deputy who was helping, came across some sheets of metal across the bottom of the pit. They laboriously lifted the sheets. Underneath were more rubble and earth, but sticking up were some whitish objects which turned out to be bones. They had come across many animal bones in their search, but all the same they examined these carefully by the light of their lanterns.

'What do you think of these?' asked PC Roe, passing across some small bones.

Hilton shrugged his shoulders. 'Dunno. Small sheep or lamb?'

The policeman shook his head. 'They're from the arm of a young child.'

Soon afterwards they found some tattered clothing, which later proved to be from a small boy's trousers.

During the next few days a child's skull was discovered, a quantity of female clothing and part of the leg of an adult woman.

Eventually Dr John Stopford, Professor of Anatomy at Manchester University, was able to identify the bones as belonging to an adult woman and two children, a very young boy and an older girl.

The trial of Albert Edward Burrows, aged sixty-two, for the murder of Hannah Calladine, thirty-two, and her son Albert Edward Burrows, fifteen months, opened at the Derbyshire Assizes in Derby on 8 July 1923, before Mr Justice Shearman. The prosecution was led by Sir Henry Maddocks KC assisted by Norman Birkett, in one of his first murder trials. Burrows was defended by T. Norman Winning KC and assisted by Miss Cobb, the first time a woman barrister had appeared in a murder trial.

The evidence against Burrows was overwhelming, and the jury took only fifteen minutes to bring in a verdict of 'guilty'.* Albert Burrows was hanged on 8 August 1923, at Bagthorpe Gaol.

One of the more macabre features of the case was the evidence of a neighbour who had seen Burrows walking down the street, with the young daughter of Hannah Calladine, on the day after the disappearance of her mother and brother. When Burrows appeared, a couple of hours later, walking back up the street, he was alone. The neighbour asked him what had happened to the little girl.

'Oh,' said Burrows, 'I took Elsie to her mother.'

---

* He was then sentenced to death. In view of the verdict and sentence he was not charged with the murder of Hannah Calladine's daughter Elsie, or with the murder of Tommy Wood.

9   Albert Goozee:
An Unusual Triangle

The children's party at the house in Alexandra Road, Parkstone, a suburb of Poole in Dorset, was in full swing. They'd had the sandwiches, the lemonade, the cakes and the jellies. They'd put on the paper hats. Now they were down to the serious business of the games.

The year was 1954, and the party was for the thirteenth birthday of Norma, the youngest daughter of the Leakey family. Since she had invited most of her teenaged friends at the Parkstone Grammar School, the games were mainly variations of Postman's Knock, where couples, who were chosen at random, were supposed to kiss.

There were only two adults at the party. Mrs Lydia Margaretta Leakey, usually known as Margaret, a matronly looking housewife of fifty-three, was Norma's mother. She had two other daughters and a son, but they were grown up and no longer lived at home. The other adult was Albert William Goozee, a tall, dark, good-looking man in his early thirties, who was the new lodger.

Albert Goozee was the life and soul of the party. Far from acting like a thirty-year-old, he behaved more like a teenager himself. His jokes and imitations had all the girls screaming with laughter, and he entered fully into the swing of things, suggesting new games and variations on old ones.

No one could afterwards remember if it was he who suggested 'Spinning the Bottle' or not, but soon they were sitting round in a circle on the small living-room floor with the furniture pushed back to the walls. They each took turns to spin the empty lemonade bottle on the floor, and the person it stopped opposite won the right to spin the bottle themselves. Whoever it pointed to the second time, provided they were of the opposite sex, had then to go into the hall with the first and exchange a kiss.

Mrs Leakey had her turn, and the bottle slowed down, among shrieks and shouts, and eventually stopped opposite Albert Goozee.

'You two must go into the hall,' shrilled an excited and red-faced Norma, 'but we shall time you, to make sure you don't have too many kisses.'

Her mother laughed. 'You can all carry on with your game. Albert and I will go and get some more lemonade.'

Albert opened the door for his landlady and followed her into the darkness of the hall. Outside, she came close to him and whispered in his ear, 'You haven't paid me your forfeit yet, Albert.'

The young man was puzzled. 'Forfeit?'

He suddenly found himself enveloped by powerful arms, a soft body pressed against him, then two rather cracked lips crushed against his. He was so surprised that he didn't know what to do. Mrs Leakey put her head on his chest. 'I've been wanting to do that ever since you came.'

Since Albert had been there only a fortnight, he hadn't realized this and was rather embarrassed. 'Don't you think we ought to go into the kitchen and see to the lemonade?'

'Oh, don't be hard on me, Albert. I'm a very lonely woman, and my husband doesn't care about me. Just kiss me again. Just once more. Please.'

Albert Goozee didn't want to kiss her. She was old enough to be his mother. If he had to kiss anybody, he would sooner have kissed Norma. But, on the other hand, she was his landlady and he didn't want to upset her. He bent his head to her waiting lips.

When Albert went to bed that night, the excitement of the party had still not subsided in him. He remembered the laughter of the young girls, their sparkling eyes and their white limbs. He was just drifting off with the memory of young Norma, encouraged by her mother, dancing a Scottish reel and her skirt flying up as she whirled around, when he felt a hand on his shoulder.

'Albert,' came a hoarse whisper. It was the voice of Mrs Leakey.

He sat up in bed immediately. 'Whatever's the matter?'

'Sh … Keep your voice down. Someone may hear.'

She then began to tell him again how lonely she was and how her husband was a coarse beast and that for the past eight years she had had to share a bedroom with Norma while her husband slept in the back room. She came close to him, and in the darkness he could feel her body through her nightdress and smell the perfume she had put on.

'Can I come into your bed for a while? It's cold out here.'

'You can't! What if your husband hears you?'

'He sleeps like a log. He won't hear a thing. Please. Just for a little while.' She pulled back the clothes on the double bed and slipped in beside him. Her body was warm against his. Soon she slipped her arms about him and her lips found his. The excitement of the party awakened answering passions in him, and he found himself responding to her kisses.

After they'd made love, she lay close beside him. 'Darling, that was wonderful. You don't know what it means to me.'

Suddenly the bedroom door opened. 'Mum? Is that you in there?' It was the soft, urgent, whisper of the thirteen-year-old Norma.

Albert jerked away from Margaret.

'Mum!' came the young girl's insistent whisper. Her young eyes pierced the darkness of the room. 'What are you doing in bed with Albert?'

There was a sharp intake of breath from her mother, and when Margaret's voice came, it was dry and scratchy. 'Go back to bed, Norma.'

'Are you all right?' The young girl approached the bed.

'Yes, yes. You go back and I'll tell you about it in the morning.'

But Norma, with the important milestone of her thirteenth birthday behind her and a new-found independence, was not to be put off so easily. She sat on the edge of the bed.

'Why have you come into Albert's bed in the middle of the night?'

'Norma! I shan't tell you again. Go back to bed!'

Albert sat up. He was on the side nearer Norma. 'Sh, you two,' he said in a hissing whisper. 'You'll wake the whole house.'

'Well, she's got to … '

'Sh.' This time he put his hand over Margaret's mouth. 'Let her get into bed with us. Just for a short time.'

Margaret hesitated. 'Only for a minute,' she said reluctantly. 'Then she must go back to bed.'

The young Norma needed no second invitation. She slipped into bed alongside Albert. She was wearing a new nighty, which had been a birthday present, and, still retaining some of the innocence of the very young, she cuddled up to Albert, wrapping both arms and legs around him.

'You smell of Mum's perfume,' she said sleepily.

Albert said nothing. He was in Heaven.

Although he was in his early thirties, Albert Goozee related far more easily to the young than to older people. His family had been dispersed when he was young, and he had been brought up in an institution. When he left, he joined the Merchant Navy and served throughout the war. On discharge he had come to Poole to look up his brother. Since then he'd had a succession of jobs and at the time he went to live with the Leakeys was a fitter's mate.

The relationship with Mrs Leakey and her daughter continued. The middle-aged woman would come to his room frequently at night and climb into bed with him. Albert couldn't help making love to her, although his strict upbringing ensured that he was tortured by guilt at what he was doing.

Often the scene after the party would be repeated, and Norma would follow her mother into his bed. Sometimes she arrived so quickly that she interrupted their love-making, and Albert would then have to pacify them both, occasionally continuing to make love to Margaret while her daughter lay by their side.

During the day Mrs Leakey treated Albert some way between a lover and a son. She would ask him what he wanted for his meals, a privilege which she apparently never offered her husband. Rarely would she take the £2 rent every week, and she would always give him small sums if he asked. She gave him money for a car, supplying at least half the £95 he spent on it and even persuading her husband to contribute £5.

Thomas Leakey, a one-legged veteran of the First World War, was a wood-machine operator in a factory. He reached home at about seven each evening and by 8.30 was in the pub. He seemed to spend most of his spare time in the Retreat Hotel in Parkstone and the Branksome Conservative Club, where he was the domino champion. He was undoubtedly afraid of the stronger and far more aggressive young man, and if he noticed the nights his wife spent in Goozee's bed or the attention she paid him, he didn't mention it.

The situation with Norma was rather different. Whereas Margaret centred her interest on Albert, he lavished affection on the young girl. He bought her records and cheap jewellery and took her out in the car more than he did her mother.

One evening, when he had driven Norma to Salisbury, about thirty miles away, his car broke down in the town and they could not get back that night. Representing himself as the girl's father, he booked a double room in a hotel, and that night they shared a bed without Mrs Leakey.

This state of affairs seemed to continue placidly for some months, but under the surface it was far from calm. Albert Goozee simply hadn't the emotional equipment to cope with the situation. Seduced by Margaret Leakey, he was infatuated with Norma. Excited by sex, he was beset by feelings of guilt and remorse. He became subject to wild swings of mood, and the violence of his temper would flare up at the slightest provocation.

One day there was a row between Mr and Mrs Leakey. The next morning, when Mrs Leakey had gone downstairs to get the breakfast ready, Albert went into Tom's bedroom.

'I've sorted things out for you, Tom.'

'What are you talking about?'

'With Margaret. The row you had yesterday. I've managed to calm her down.'

Perhaps it was the arrogance of this which finally caused Thomas Leakey to decide to stand up for himself. He hobbled, on his stick, round the side of the bed and faced the much taller man, glaring up at him.

'It's got nothing to do with you! And I'll thank you to stop messing about with my wife and daughter.'

But he got no further, for Goozee suddenly lashed out, and Tom went backwards onto the bed, sliding across it and crashing into a table on the other side. He howled in pain as he tumbled to the floor and cringed as the younger man came round the bed and stood over him.

'Help!' yelled Leakey. 'Help me, someone! He's going to kill me!'

There was a pounding up the stairs, and Margaret burst

into the room.

'Albert! For God's sake, Albert! Leave him alone!' She grabbed the young man's arm and dragged him away.

He allowed her to lead him from the room. Then he shook her off and went downstairs. When the other two came down later, it was to find that he had gone off to work.

Thomas Leakey had had enough. The next day he packed a bag and left, taking the train to Andover, where his sister lived. When Albert came home that night, it was to find Mrs Leakey sitting at the table with a very long face.

'Tom's gone to his sister's,' she announced.

'Good thing, I should think,' said the young man, picking up the evening paper and sitting by the fire in Leakey's chair.

'Don't be stupid,' snapped Margaret. 'We can't live on your wages. I've a young daughter to support. She's going to need a new school blazer soon, and she goes through shoes like nobody's business. Tomorrow we'll have to drive up there and try to persuade Tom to come back home.'

Albert's answer was a shouted tirade against Tom.

But the next day Margaret, Norma and Albert set out for Andover in the car. They were received by Tom's sister with a stony face.

'I don't want any trouble here,' she said as she let them in. 'This is a respectable house.'

'There's going to be no trouble,' said Mrs Leakey. 'We just want to talk to Tom.'

They talked in the front sitting-room. But very soon an argument developed and Goozee lost his temper.

'You're telling lies about me and your daughter,' he shouted. 'Well, you know what happened last time!'

'You mean, when you took advantage of a man with only one leg?'

'I hit you last time. Next time I'll kill you!'

Norma screamed and cowered in a corner. Tom's sister picked up a poker. 'You get out of here! Norma, you go for the police.'

'No, Auntie, no! Don't send for the police! He'll kill us all if you do!'

But Tom's sister was not overawed by Albert. She advanced on him with the poker in her hand. 'Out you go!'

Albert Goozee left hurriedly. He drove off in the car and went back to Parkstone, expecting that Mrs Leakey and her daughter would soon follow. But they didn't.

A few days later he received a letter from Margaret. It was apologetic in tone but said quite plainly that she was going to stay with her husband. She also said that Tom would return home only if Albert left and that consequently the young man would have to find himself somewhere else to live.

It came as a shock to Goozee but also as somewhat of a relief. At least now he would be free of the millstone of guilt he had carried for the past eighteen months or so.

He obtained new lodgings in Parkstone, and for a few days he felt like a new man. But then all the old yearnings and longings returned, and to make matters worse he began to receive letters from Mrs Leakey.

'Dear Albert. Please come back home. I will just be a mother to you. I would be so happy just to do your cooking and washing and ironing. Think of what comfort you have had for £2 a week … Just let me see to you, anyway, until you decide to get married.' That letter and others like it threw Albert into turmoil. He felt pulled back by his pent-up desires and yet pressed down by his feelings of guilt.

He went to the pictures, at a Bournemouth cinema, alone one night and found himself sitting next to a young girl. In the darkness her limbs took on the shape of Norma's, and he could not resist putting his hand on her leg. She screamed and Albert was seized by a large man sitting on the other side of her, who turned out to be her father, and carted off to the manager's office. He was charged with indecent assault, appeared at Bournemouth Magistrates' Court on the morning of Saturday 16 June and was remanded on bail to appear the following Wednesday.

Albert Goozee left the court and went back to his lodgings convinced that he had reached the depths of degradation. He had become a pervert, a despoiler of adolescents. When the case came up on Wednesday and the story came out, he would be unable to face his brother, his workmates or the Leakey family. The only possible course open to him was to end it all before then.

But, like a lot of would-be suicides, he wanted to tell someone all about it. He couldn't think of any friends or relatives to whom he would care to unburden himself so, since the police would take charge of his body when it was found, he decided to write to the Chief Constable of Bournemouth.

Goozee began writing the letter on Saturday and finished it on Sunday morning. As he related the progress of his relationship with Mrs Leakey and her daughter, he began to think that Margaret and Norma were really responsible for the position in which he found himself.

'Norma,' he wrote, 'has made me into a sex maniac. Mrs Leakey still goes after me, so I have come to the only possible way out before I go after another young girl.'

After his dinner on Sunday he put the letter in the car, together with the communication from Mrs Leakey telling him that her husband had insisted he should leave, and a letter from her asking him to come back. These would back up his story to the Chief Constable.

He told his landlady that he was feeling rather queasy and was going to drive to the New Forest, a few miles away, to get some air. Instead he drove to Alexandra Road.

Margaret Leakey was pleased to see him.

'Is your husband around?' he asked after a while.

Mrs Leakey shook her head. 'Tom's taken the dog for a walk.'

'Fancy a drive to the New Forest?'

'What a lovely idea! I'll cut some sandwiches and we'll have a picnic.'

'Can we take Norma?'

'If you like. I think she's doing her homework in the kitchen. Norma! Do you want to come on a picnic?'

'Tell you what,' said Albert. 'We'll take an axe and chop some wood for a fire.'

'Quite the boy scout, aren't we?' Margaret slipped her arm around him and gave him a hug. 'Come on, Norma. See if you can help me find the axe. I think it's out in the woodshed.'

While they went into the garden, Albert opened a kitchen drawer and took out Mrs Leakey's son's commando knife, which he slipped into his pocket.

They drove north-west until they came to the New Forest.

'There's some nice places in Bignell Wood,' said Mrs Leakey.

They drove along the Cadman to Brook road until Albert spotted a track leading off into the wood. He turned the car into it, and they drove for over half a mile into the forest, with the overhanging trees touching the top and sides of the car. Then a clearing opened out on the right.

'This'll be all right,' said Albert stopping the car. He got out and looked around. They were almost fully enclosed by trees, and the only sound they could hear was that of birdsong. It was the ideal spot.

'You go and pick some bluebells, Norma. Albert and I will make the fire.' Mrs Leakey put her arm round his waist, leaned her head on his shoulder and whispered: 'We'll make the fire afterwards … '

At about five o'clock that evening the dishevelled figure of

Albert Goozee was seen by motorists by the side of the Cadman to Brook road. He was covered in blood and had a knife wound in the stomach. He was taken to hospital, and the police were called. They searched the forest and found two bodies, that of Mrs Leakey and Norma.

Margaret Leakey had head wounds, caused no doubt by the axe which was found underneath the bodies, and two stab wounds, one in the abdomen, the other in the groin. The young girl had a broken jaw and a stab wound to the heart.

Goozee, whose stomach wound was not serious, told a series of conflicting stories. He said that Mrs Leakey had stabbed him first. He had pulled out the dagger and attacked both of them, 'She knew I was seducing her daughter,' he added.

He later told a complicated story involving his having intercourse with Mrs Leakey, and Norma appearing and hitting her mother over the head with an axe as she lay on top of him. He then struck Norma, and later Mrs Leakey stabbed him. He retaliated by stabbing her and later the young girl.

Albert Goozee was tried for the murder of Norma Leakey only, at the Hampshire Assizes on Monday 3 December 1956, before Mr Justice Havers. Norman Fox-Andrews QC prosecuted, and Goozee was defended by Robert Hughes QC. In the witness box he changed his story yet again and said that he had not stabbed Norma. When he was struggling with Mrs Leakey for the knife, after he had been wounded, Norma had tried to come between them and was herself pierced by the weapon.

The jury, after deliberating for 3½ hours, found the prisoner guilty. After the verdict Mr Justice Havers directed that the indictment relating to the alleged murder of Mrs Leakey should remain on the file marked 'Not to be proceeded with without the direction of the Court'. Albert Goozee was duly sentenced to death, but was later reprieved.

During the trial it was revealed that the post-mortem showed that Norma had been a virgin. Goozee had never had intercourse with her at all.

10   Ronald Harries:
'Gone on Holiday'

It was a dark night in October 1953. Along the quiet lanes of Carmarthenshire sped a Landrover. Its headlights picked out the high banks and hedgerows on either side as it swept round the corners of the narrow, twisting roads which are a feature of that part of the country. But it met no one, for in those days there were not many vehicles on the roads of South Wales.

After rounding a bend in the undulating road, the driver changed down and the vehicle slowed. The two passengers cramped inside said nothing as the Landrover, now almost at walking pace, turned into a gap in the bank on the left. There was a roar as the driver revved to take the incline in front, then the noise of the engine petered out and the vehicle juddered to a halt.

'You had it in too high a gear,' said the elderly man sitting in the Landrover.

'No,' said the driver crossly, 'it often stalls at low revvs.' He got out and there was a clanking sound as he lifted the bonnet. 'Come and look at this,' he said shining a torch into the engine.

The older man slowly climbed out of the vehicle.

On Saturday 17 October 1953 Rowland James, who lived near the small hilltop village of Llangynin, some twelve miles from Carmarthen, rose early. He cycled through the village until he reached a smallholding, with its farmhouse on the roadside, called Derlwyn, the home of Mr and Mrs John Harries. Since Rowland James had a week's holiday from his job on the railways, he had promised to go ferreting with Mr Harries.

James tapped at the back door, because nobody ever used the front, but there was no answer. Although it was only 8.30 in the morning, he knew that John Harries would be up, because he normally milked his five cows at seven o'clock. He shouted: 'Mr Harries!' and then: 'Mrs Harries!' but there was no reply.

He walked across to the cowshed and saw that the floor was still dry, which indicated that the cows had not yet been milked. This was confirmed when he opened the door, as the beasts inside started bellowing, anxious to be relieved of their milk.

Puzzled, he got back on his bicycle and went home. Later he called on his brother, Jestyn, who lived nearby, and together they returned to Derlwyn, arriving at about eleven o'clock in the morning. There was still nobody about, but the cows had by that time been milked, and two churns stood by the roadside ready for collection. It was all very odd.

The James brothers had known John Harries and his wife since they were children, and they were surprised that the couple seemed to have gone away and not told them where they were going. Conversations with neighbours confirmed that somebody was looking after the smallholding. Some people had noticed a young man there at times, who appeared to be driving the Harrieses' car, a fairly new Austin A40.

Jestyn James was accustomed to go to Derlwyn several times a week, and he next went on the following Monday morning. The first thing he saw was the A40 car parked by the side of the house. He walked round the back, towards the chicken house, and saw a young man come out of the shed with some eggs in his hands. He was in his twenties, not very tall, but handsome, with black wavy hair and dark eyes.

'Is Mr Harries there?'

'No,' said the young man shortly and pushed passed him to take his eggs into a porch at the back of the house.

Jestyn James waited patiently for him to come out again. 'You'll be … ?' he queried. He had seen the young man around the place before, but he was not going to let him know that.

'I'm Ronnie Harries, but people call me Ronnie Cadno because I used to live at Cadno Farm, near Pendine.'

Jestyn James nodded his head. He knew that Pendine was a little village on the coast some twelve miles away, well known in South Wales as a seaside resort with an unrivalled stretch of golden sands which in the 1920s had been used for attempts on the world land speed record. James had also heard of Cadno Farm, home of Mr and Mrs John Lloyd Harries, presumably the parents of Ronnie Harries and relatives of the Harrieses of Derlwyn.

The young man confirmed this. 'The old chap here is my uncle, see?'

Jestyn James guessed that this could not be strictly true. Ronnie Harries was more likely to be a distant cousin. But he said nothing, for now the ice had been broken the young man seemed anxious to talk.

'Auntie and uncle are having a holiday at Cadno, and they asked me to keep an eye on the place.' He took out a packet of cigarettes and, without offering the older man one, lit up and puffed away at it quickly. 'He has his potato-digger at Cadno and is helping to dig some down there.'

James realized that this could well be true, as John Harries had enough equipment on his eleven-acre holding to stock a much larger farm and was always lending it out to farmers in the district.

'Did you want something?' asked Ronnie Harries.

'Not really. I often pop in for a chat with John. But he did say I could borrow a pig net as I've to fetch a pig from Carmarthen. I think the net's in the garage.'

The young man produced a bunch of keys, but none of them would open the garage door. 'I'll get the right one off him later today and leave the net out for you tomorrow,' he said as he got into John Harries's car. 'It's quite a nice car he's got himself now, isn't it?' He drove off.

But the next day the pig net was not there.

The sudden disappearance of the Harrieses was also causing concern in the village. John Harries had an arrangement to collect waste food every day from the kitchen of the village school, which was next door to his holding, for use as animal feed. But after Friday it was not collected at all, and by Wednesday it was piling up so much that the schoolmaster had to make other arrangements to get rid of it.

Simon Phillips, an agricultural merchant, who was the brother-in-law of John Harries, was expecting a telephone call from him on Saturday, but he never received it. He didn't get one on Sunday, Monday or Tuesday. By Tuesday evening he and his wife were becoming worried, and they called at Derlwyn. The place was shut up and dark.

The next day, in company with another brother-in-law, Lawrence Davies, he went again to Derlwyn. They saw Ronnie Harries in a field, and Lawrence Davies recognized him as the young man he had seen with John Harries a few days earlier, when they came to collect a potato-digger from him.

They called to him, 'Where are the Harrieses?'

'Oh, they've gone on their holidays to London,' said Ronnie Harries, walking across to them.

'To London?' said Lawrence Davies in surprise. 'Why, he's never been to London in his life. And he's sixty-three now. I can't see him going that far!'

'Well, he has,' said Harries doggedly. 'He told me they'd not had a holiday for eight years, and this year they were going to. I drove them down to Carmarthen on Saturday morning. We had a cup of tea in the Willow Café, then I drove them to the station.' He lit a cigarette. 'He told me they were going to catch a train for London and would be away for a week or ten days. He didn't say where they were going to stay, but he said he would write to me. He said I could use his car, and he gave me £5 to cover my expenses.'

'Very generous, I'm sure,' said Phillips. 'What's happened to his cows?'

'I've taken them to Cadno. I had trouble getting them into the cowshed here.'

'I don't know much about cows,' replied Phillips, 'but I always understood they would go into their own shed better than a strange one.'

'I know you must be upset, because you are related to Mr Harries and he has asked me to look after the place, without telling you, but it's not my fault. I'm doing the best I can.'

The two men discussed the matter later.

'I don't believe it,' said Lawrence Davies, Mrs Harries's brother. 'Do you? They would never go off without telling anyone in the village. I'm very much afraid something has happened to them. John Harries has a brother who lives in Reading. I'm going to get in touch with him. Then I'm going to the police.'

The police soon discovered that Ronald Harries was a married man, with a baby daughter, who lived with his wife's parents at Ashwell Farm, Pendine, no more than a few minutes walk from his parents' farm. His in-laws didn't see much of him, however, because for most of the day he delivered meat for his father, who was a butcher as well as a farmer, and took all his meals at Cadno.

At about six in the evening on Thursday 22 October, Detective Constable Thomas Lamford called at Ashwell

Farm and asked Ronald Harries if he would go with him to Derlwyn. The young man agreed and after picking up the keys at Cadno took the Constable to Derlwyn in his father's Landrover.

There they saw Superintendent William Lloyd, who was in charge of the Carmarthen Police. In the small sitting-room of the farmhouse, with its cooking-range and fire on one side of the room, they sat round the table. Superintendent Lloyd asked Ronald Harries what he knew of the movements of Mr and Mrs Harries on the evening of Friday the 16th.

The young man scratched his head, then lit the inevitable cigarette. He blew a cloud of smoke into the room.

'From what auntie and uncle said, they went to the Harvest Thanksgiving Service at Bryn Chapel, just down the road from here.'

'Do you know what time they got back home?' asked the Superintendent.

'They told me it was about 8.30.'

'And what time did you actually see them?'

'I suppose it must have been a few minutes later. When I arrived, they had a neighbour with them, a Mr Morris. My uncle was speaking to me in English, while auntie was talking to Mr Morris in Welsh. Then he left. I had to back my Landrover to let him get his car out. I went soon afterwards. Just before I left, uncle reminded me to be sure to come between ten and half-past the next morning to drive them to Carmarthen to catch the train.'

'What did you do after you'd left your uncle and auntie that evening?'

'Well, on a Friday night I usually collect my father from the Beach Hotel at about ten o'clock, see? My mother goes to see a friend at Edith Villas, near Pendine, and I pick her up at 10.30. But as I was driving towards Pendine I met George Wilson on the road. He was having some trouble with his car, and I gave him a tow to where he lives – well, to the gateway of Middle Pool Farm.'

'What time would that be?'

'I'm not sure. But it made me late picking up my father and mother. About 10.30 it was then.'

He went on to repeat the same story, about taking Mr and Mrs Harries to Carmarthen on the Saturday morning, that he had told to Phillips and Davies earlier in the week.

The police searched the Derlwyn farmhouse and made some interesting discoveries. In the bathroom they found some working clothes lying on the floor. This pointed to John Harries' having changed his clothes, possibly to go to a Harvest Thanksgiving Service, but not to his having gone on holiday. Mrs Harries was too tidy a woman to have left her husband's clothes lying about like that if they were going away for any length of time.

The cooking was done on the range in the living-room, and in its oven they found a joint of meat covered with grease-proof paper – again, surely an indication that the couple had not intended to be away for long.

Checking on the young man's story, the police went to the Willow Café in Carmarthen. The same waitress was there as on the Saturday morning in question, but she didn't remember seeing either Ronald Harries on that particular morning or Mr and Mrs Harries. And the ticket-collector at the railway station did not remember the couple getting on a train either.

The young man's story was sounding thinner and thinner. Then came some evidence which blew it apart altogether.

The police found Brian Powell, a boy of fifteen, who lived with his mother at Pendine. He had often helped out at Cadno Farm and knew Ronnie Harries well. On the Saturday morning Harries called for him at 8.30 and drove him to Derlwyn, telling the boy that his (Ronnie's) uncle and aunt had gone on holiday and he was in charge of the smallholding. Together they milked the cows and fed the stock, all at the time when Harries said he was driving his uncle and aunt to Carmarthen to see them off on the train.

Then the manager of John Harries's bank in St Clears, the nearest town to the village of Llangynin, received a cheque drawn on the account of the missing farmer. It was for £909, which rather surprised the bank manager, because John Harries had only £123 in his account. On inspection it appeared that the cheque had originally been for £9 but had been altered. The farmer habitually left the top line of the figures section of his cheques blank, and someone had merely filled in the words 'Nine hundred and', and then altered the figures themselves.

The cheque had been made out to Ronnie Harries's father, but it had passed through the son's hands, and he had paid in the altered cheque, asking for £500 to be paid into his father's account and £300 to his own. When the young man was questioned about it, he claimed that his uncle had made the alterations himself and that the cheque was a repayment for a loan he had previously made to his uncle.

It was an unlikely story, especially since Ronald Harries's account was in the red by about £300. But the young man stuck to it, as he did to the rest of his explanations.

Harries came under considerable pressure, not only from the police but also from a large number of relatives and friends of the missing couple, who were continually accosting him and asking what he had done with them. But he refused to change his story or to give any clue as to what had happened to the farmer and his wife.

The search for the Harrieses went on for several weeks. Disused mine shafts in the area were examined, and fishermen scanned the coastline to see if the bodies had been dumped in a secluded cove. It was rumoured that the couple had been swallowed by the quicksands on Pendine beach and would never be found.

Over eighty square miles of countryside were searched. Teams of farmers and farm-workers, police and troops scoured the hillsides, rivers and streams, while the rest of the country looked on and waited. The *News of the World* newspaper offered a £500 reward for information leading to the discovery of the Harrieses.

The Chief Constable of the Carmarthenshire Constabulary, Hubert Lewis, had by this time called in Scotland Yard, and Superintendent John Capstick and Detective Sergeant Heddon had gone to Carmarthen. Newspaper reports of the time show pictures of the spare, bowler-hatted figure of Capstick with his pipe in his mouth.

After several days interviewing local farmers and studying the statements which the police had already taken from a large number of people, Capstick talked to Superintendent William Lloyd in the latter's office.

'There's this couple,' said Capstick, 'the Wilsons of Middle Pool Farm, Pendine – the chap Ronald Harries is supposed to have given a tow on the Friday night. They've known him for some years, and they both say that he told them some time ago that he was going to dig a well on Cadno Farm. Don't you think that was just a blind in case anyone actually saw him digging? What he was really doing was preparing a grave for his aunt and uncle?'

'That may well be,' said his opposite number in the Carmarthen Force, 'but we can't dig up every inch of the Cadno place. It's far too big.'

'No,' said the Scotland Yard man, puffing at his pipe. 'Perhaps we won't have to. Didn't you tell me that Ronnie Harries is now sleeping at Cadno Farm? Now here's the plan … '

That night the police surrounded Cadno Farm. They closed off all the field entrances and gaps in the hedges with black cotton, setting the threads waist high so that dogs and other small animals could get through, while a man would break the cotton. Then they revved up a car engine in the road outside the farm. A light soon went on in one of the upper windows of the farmhouse. The police crept away.

They were back again at first light. At one field entrance, quite near where the farm track met the road, the threads were broken. Inside was a field of kale. The police meticulously examined the ground in the slowly increasing light. In one corner the soil looked as if it might have been disturbed. The plants there were not so big as others nearby.

They began to dig, slowly and carefully. Only a short distance down they came across some clothing, and then the bodies.

Mrs Harries's body was on top of her husband's. Both had their outside clothes on, as if they had been going on a visit. When the post-mortems were done, it was revealed that they had died from severe head injuries which must have been inflicted with a blunt instrument, probably a hammer. The ferocity of the blows had resulted in John Harries's skull being literally smashed in from the rear. Mrs Harries's head injuries were less severe but quite sufficient to be fatal. Death must have followed quite quickly after the attack, and both bodies had been buried soon after death.

Ronald Harries, aged twenty-five, was brought to trial on Monday 8 March 1954 at Carmarthen Assizes, before Mr Justice Havers. Edmund Davies QC, Recorder of Cardiff, prosecuted, and Harries was defended by Vincent Lloyd Jones QC, Recorder of Chester.

A wealth of witnesses were brought by the prosecution to prove that Harries's story was untrue but, with an arrogance which characterized his whole attitude, he claimed they were all telling lies. And he maintained his position all through the trial. The jury did not believe him, however, and found him guilty. He was sentenced to death. His counsel appealed against the verdict, but the appeal was dismissed, on 12 April, and Harries was executed at HM Prison, Swansea at 9 a.m. on Wednesday 28 April 1954.

One of the witnesses at the trial, Hubert Gwyn Lewis,

described how on the day before the murder he was mending a ferret box outside his house when Ronald Harries arrived with the Sunday joint of meat.

'That's a fine hammer you've got there, Gwyn.'

'Yes, it is, isn't it? I borrowed it from work to do some jobs.'

'Do you think I could borrow it?'

'I should think so, if you promise to bring it back.'

'Bring it back tomorrow without fail.'

'What do you want it for, Ronnie?'

'For a good, heavy job. It'll be just the thing for the job.'

11   Michael Copeland:
'I Hate Things Like That'

The cyclist gratefully freewheeled down the slight incline. Ahead the road, called Clod Hall Lane, rose arrow straight until it crossed the main Baslow to Sheffield road and then on beyond that to the steep rise of Curbar Edge, just north of Chatsworth Park. He was glad of the respite, not having for once to pedal up the long inclines of the Peak District near Chesterfield. It was early on the afternoon of Sunday 11 June 1960.

He was still watching the main road crossing up ahead when, out of the corner of his eye, he saw a dark shape on the grass verge. It was on his right, and a more direct glance had him applying the brakes of his bike precipitously.

It was undoubtedly a man, face down on the grass, close to the drystone wall. He might well have been asleep were it not for the dark stain on the grass which surrounded his head like a halo. The cyclist got off for a closer look and then wished he hadn't. The man's head had been terribly battered, and he had been dead a few hours.

The Chesterfield Police, when they arrived some time later, were not all that surprised. They'd been looking for a badly injured man since early that day.

In the small hours of Sunday morning a man living in Park Road, Chesterfield, had heard a crash outside his house. Looking out of the window, he saw that a two-seater bubble car – a very small car quite popular in those days – had collided with a lamp-post and was now lying on its side in the road. The police found that the upholstery was covered in blood and there were blood splashes on the windows. Inside were a set of lower dentures, a pair of shoes and a heavily bloodstained mackintosh. But the car was empty of occupants.

The dead man was soon identified as the owner of the Isetta bubble car. He was William Arthur Elliott, a sixty-year-old bachelor who lived with his two unmarried sisters in Bakewell and worked at nearby Thornbridge Hall. He had been seen in various pubs in Chesterfield on Saturday night, one of them being the Three Horse Shoes in Parker's Row.

The post-mortem showed that he had been the victim of a brutal attack and that the head injuries from which he had died could well have been inflicted by a boot.

The following Thursday evening a young couple were walking home from a wood at Engine Hollow, near Chesterfield. She was a dark, pretty girl of sixteen, and he a tall man of twenty-one, Michael Copeland. He was doing his National Service with the Royal Corps of Signals in Germany, and at the time was home on leave.

Never a very talkative young man, this evening he had been unusually quiet. The girl, who was holding his hand, stopped and put her arms around him. She looked up. 'Don't you like me any more after what happened in the wood?'

He bent and kissed the top of her head absentmindedly. 'Of course I do. It was lovely.'

'Well, why are you so quiet, then?'

Michael said nothing for some time. Then he suddenly extricated himself from her arms and stood in front of her. 'Take a good look at me!'

She was well used to his dramatic gestures. 'Why?' she asked cautiously.

'Because the next time you see me I might be swinging on the gallows!'

This was a bit much even for Michael Copeland. 'Don't be ridiculous,' she snapped. All the same, she thought he was unnaturally pale, and she remembered that he had been very nervous and jumpy all evening.

'Don't you believe me?'

'I don't think it's funny, talk like that.' His face had a peculiar look which gave her an odd feeling in her stomach.

'What would you say if I told you I'd murdered a man at Birdholme?'

She knew that Birdholme was a part of Chesterfield very near where he lived. But she didn't want to go along with his fantasies. 'I would tell you not to talk silly!'

He stood looking at her, and his eyes seemed to burn into her. Then he turned away and walked on. She stood for a moment, not knowing quite what to do. Then she rushed after him and grabbed his arm. 'Michael! You're not … serious?'

He laughed in her face. 'Don't you think I'm a good actor? You didn't believe me, did you?'

But his denial was worse, if anything, than his confession, because it sounded so false.

She spent a sleepless night. Could Michael's words be true or was he just play-acting? She knew he was normally a rather withdrawn person, who loved the quiet of the countryside. Of an artistic temperament, he could draw and paint well and wrote poetry. But he was subject to wild rages which could blow up without the least warning, and in one of those – well, he was big and strong enough to kill someone almost by accident.

The next day she went to the police. They subsequently called at Copeland's home at 6.20 in the morning and asked him to go to the police station. He was kept there until ten o'clock that night.

Michael Copeland was well known to the Chesterfield Police. He'd left school when he was fifteen and gone down the pit as a haulage hand. But it was not long before he was in trouble. In 1956, when he was seventeen, he was convicted of housebreaking and being in possession of a firearm. Then twice the following year he was convicted of housebreaking, theft and burglary, and in each case he was given Borstal training.

Although Copeland was only one of some 15,000 men interviewed in the police investigation of what became known as 'the Bubble Car Murder', he was a promising suspect. His home was quite near Park Road, where the car had been abandoned, and a witness was found who had seen him in a chip shop near where the car had been left, at about midnight. Copeland had had blood on his hands and on his shirt.

The police surmised that whoever had murdered William Elliott had used the bubble car to take the body to Clod Hall Lane, out on the moors, and then driven the car back into Chesterfield to dump it near where he lived.

But there was absolutely nothing to connect Copeland and Elliott. There was no evidence that they even knew each other, and no one had ever seen them together. Michael Copeland did not have an alibi for the Saturday night, but nor did a lot of the men interviewed. And careful examination of his clothes, in particular his boots, showed no traces of anything which would connect him with the crime.

Michael Copeland went back to Germany.

13 November 1960 was a Sunday. In the small town of Verden, on the River Aller, near Münster, Günther Helmbrecht, who was two days off being sixteen years old, took his fifteen-year-old girlfriend Inge Hoppe to the pictures. They saw the film *Rebecca* at the Regina Cinema in the street called Lindhoopstrasse. The programme finished at ten minutes to nine in the evening, and they decided to go for a walk in the forest near the town.

The forest began on the outskirts, near the Caithness Army Barracks, one of the bases of the Royal Corps of Signals in Germany. The young couple walked into the wood until they came to a small hut, a well-known rendezvous for lovers. And in fact there was another couple there when they arrived, whom they knew, Adolf Struver and his girlfriend. They waited until Adolf and his girlfriend went off to catch a bus and then went into the hut themselves.

After some time they saw a man approaching. It was quite dark in the forest, with only the moon giving a pale light through the trees, so they couldn't see him very easily, but he appeared to be in British Army uniform. He looked into the hut and then went and stood by a tree some thirty feet away, watching them.

'I'm frightened,' said Inge.

'No need to be,' replied Günther.

'I think we ought to go,' said the girl.

Günther looked out of the hut at the man, who was tall and well built, far bigger than he was. 'Perhaps we'd better walk on.'

They made their way down the path, hand in hand, through the trees, until they came out into a clearing. Suddenly Inge could hear the sound of footfalls following them, thudding quickly on the frozen ground.

'Hurry!' she urged her boyfriend, pulling him along by the arm.

But still the hurrying footsteps came on. Inge risked a look over her shoulder and saw the dark bulk of the big man almost upon them. She pulled Günther's arm, drawing him away so that the stranger could pass them on the narrow path. But he didn't pass. She could see his long arm swing out as he came abreast, and it caught Günther on the neck. Her boyfriend gave a strangled cry and dropped her hand. Inge screamed. It seemed as if it would be her turn next. She raced away down the path. Behind her she could hear shouts and yells and the sound of blows in the frosty night air. But she didn't look back. She ran as fast as she could until she came out onto the main road, the Lindhoopstrasse, gasping for breath.

There were four boys walking along, and she knew the name of one of them was Hans-Dieter Varrelmann. She gasped out her story. Then along came Adolf Struver, who had been waiting at the bus stop with his girlfriend and had heard the commotion.

'We must go back into the forest,' he told Inge, 'and see if we can help Günther.'

He and Varrelmann persuaded a reluctant Inge to go back into the dark wood with them. They soon lost their way but after wandering around in the gloom for some time eventually found the hut. Then Inge was able to show them the direction she and Günther had taken a while before. When they came out into the clearing, they saw, in the fitful moonlight, Günther lying on the ground. He was unconscious and bleeding from several stab wounds to the chest.

'We must try and get him to the road,' said Struver.

Together they half dragged, half carried the unconscious teenager back to the main road, where Inge phoned for help. But when the police and ambulance men arrived, Günther was already dead.

The post-mortem showed that the boy had twenty-seven stab wounds in his body, three of which had penetrated the heart.

That same night Michael Copeland, who was a driver with the Royal Corps of Signals, stationed at the Caithness Barracks, staggered into the guardroom bleeding from a deep knife wound in his leg. He said he'd been attacked by two German civilians (an occurrence not unknown in Germany in those days) near a pub. He was taken to hospital to have his wound dressed but was not detained.

Copeland, obviously a suspect in the murder of the German boy, underwent three identification parades. He was then interviewed by Captain Hubert Lambert of the Army Special Investigations Branch.

'We can't find any evidence for your story that you were attacked by two civilians,' said the Captain.

'I didn't expect you to believe me.'

'We've been over the spot you pointed out, with a fine-tooth comb.'

Copeland shrugged his shoulders. 'There've been that many men tramping over those woods, I'm surprised there's anything left to find.'

'They've been trying to find evidence of the killer of the young German boy.'

Copeland studied his fingernails. 'Nothing to do with me.'

'Did you know that the morning after the boy was stabbed the German police took a specially trained police dog down to the spot where the stabbing took place? It circled the area and then made straight for the camp, here. Near the piggery there's a hole in the perimeter fence, and the dog followed the scent right through into the camp. That means it's very likely that the person who stabbed the boy is resident here.'

'There's hundreds of men on this camp – could have been any one of them. I've been on three identification parades now, and no one has picked me out. Sounds to me as if you ought to be looking for someone else.'

The German Police and the British Military Police used mine-detectors to search for the knife which had been used to stab Günther Helmbrecht – even the camp sewers were emptied and searched. But, although several hundred knives were found in the camp, the weapon which was used to kill the German teenager was not discovered. There was nothing to link the tall soldier with the murder of the German boy.

Copeland continued his Army service and during 1961 completed it and returned to Chesterfield. He obtained a job as a driver at Markham Colliery.

On the morning of Wednesday 29 March 1961, at about

8.15, a lorry-driver found the body of a man on the grass verge in Clod Hall Lane. It was almost the same spot where the body of William Elliott had been found nearly a year before. And there were other similarities as well. A saloon car was found abandoned in Park Road, only a few yards away from where Mr Elliott's bubble car had been discovered, and the back seat of the saloon was bloodstained.

The car was a rare 1930 Morris Oxford, and its owner, George Gerald Stobbs, was a forty-eight-year-old industrial chemist who worked at the Trebor sweet factory in Chesterfield and he had lived in the town for less than a year.

The body, which was identified by Mrs Stobbs as that of her husband, had suffered severe head injuries, which might have been caused by a boot. The autopsy put the time of death as about twelve o'clock the previous night. The similarity to what the press had called 'the Bubble Car Murder' ensured that the Stobbs crime soon became known as 'the Carbon Copy Murder'.

Michael Copeland had been well known to newspaper reporters as a suspect in the Elliott murder, and the day after the body of George Stobbs was discovered, Jerry Dodd, Chief Reporter of the *Derbyshire Times*, called at Copeland's home. He told him what had happened, and the young man replied: 'Oh God, that means they'll be after me again!'

He was right. Officers from the Chesterfield Police arrived at his home that afternoon and invited him to go to the town police station. They also took possession of some clothes at his home and from two lockers at the Markham Colliery baths.

Again Copeland had no real alibi for the night of the murder. According to him, he had gone out alone, visited several pubs in Chesterfield and returned home before midnight. But he stoutly denied being involved in the crime.

Several days later a woman exercising her dogs, on the Stubbing Court Estate a few miles to the south of Chesterfield, was walking through Gladwin Wood when she came across a small brown diary lying on a path. Inside was the name George Stobbs, and the pages of the book were bloodstained.

The police found more of Stobbs's possessions in the wood: a fountain pen and a comb. Plainly this was where the murder had taken place. Further evidence was found that the murderer had dragged his victim a considerable distance along a path, up to a stone wall and had hoisted him over it – since the chemist was five feet ten inches tall, this was no mean feat. Presumably the killer had then loaded the body into Stobbs's car and driven out to Clod Hall Lane to dump it.

'Are you sure Copeland's our man?' asked Superintendent Rudin of the Chesterfield Town Police, at a subsequent meeting called to discuss the case.

'Pretty sure,' replied Detective Superintendent Stretton, head of Derbyshire CID. 'Tom Peat has a theory about the case. I'll let him tell you.'

Chief Inspector Thomas Peat nodded. 'I think we're all agreed that we're dealing with a sexual psychopath. The two murdered men were probably homosexuals – certainly the post-mortem on Stobbs showed that he was an active receptor homosexual. And they frequented pubs where we know men of this type meet. We know Copeland was in the same area, and he's quite possibly one of these blokes with a down on homosexuals.'

'Go on about your theory, Tom,' said Stretton.

'I think that, although he denies being concerned and he's been clever enough not to leave any evidence on his clothes, he really wants to be caught.'

'How's that?' asked Rudin.

'Well, why didn't he hide Stobbs's body in the wood, where it might have been undiscovered for weeks? Why did he drag it eighty yards, hump it over a wall, struggle it into the back of a car and drive all the way out to Clod Hall Lane? It was a terribly risky thing to do – a lot of people might have seen him. I think he did it because he wanted the body to be discovered quickly. And I think he did the same thing with Elliott.'

'He either wants to be caught or he's the most arrogant murderer I've ever come across,' said the Chief of the CID. 'But I tell you one thing. We've got to nail him soon before he kills again.'

'It's going to be difficult,' said Tom Peat. 'He's an intelligent lad and knows all about evidence and keeping his mouth shut at interviews, from his previous contacts with the police. We can try and keep him under surveillance, but we're short of men as it is.'

'We'll have to try that,' agreed Stretton, 'but it would be better if he could be persuaded to confess. See if you can play the father figure, Tom. If you say he wants to be caught, maybe he wants someone to confess to.'

'I'll do my best,' said Tom Peat.

And so he began a series of informal chats with Michael Copeland. They met in pubs and sometimes in Peat's office at the police station, and he seemed to be gaining the confidence of the young man.

But although, over the next few weeks, the Chief Inspector got on good terms with Copeland, the surveillance the young man was undergoing was having the opposite effect. Police cars were often stationed in the street where he lived, and he would be followed to and from work. When he went out at night, his footsteps might be dogged again. And if he went into a pub, a couple of plain clothes officers would very often enter soon afterwards.

In May the young man's temper erupted, and he assaulted two police officers near his home – no action was taken against him. In June the police were called to a pub in Chesterfield and found Copeland drunk and abusive. He threw a glass against the bar and struck a police sergeant on the jaw. This time he was charged with assault and, in view of his previous convictions, was sentenced to four months in prison.

When he was released, the interviewing was taken over by Inspector Bradshaw of the Chesterfield Town Police. He seemed to get along with the young man really well, and Copeland revealed to him some secrets of his early life and his obsession with the number 11 as a date. This was the date when his mother had died and when each of his dogs had died – and the date of one of the murders. The surveillance continued, and also the talks with Inspector Bradshaw, but nothing decisive to the solving of the crimes happened for another two years.

During that time, Copeland seemed to be slowly falling apart. He lost his job, fell out with his father, with whom he lived, and moved away. In November 1963 his girlfriend broke of their engagement and he was jailed in January 1964 for a vicious assault on his rival.

Late on the night of Sunday 17 November 1963, Copeland rang Bradshaw at home and said he wanted to talk to him. Bradshaw, by then a Chief Inspector, went to the office and saw Copeland.

'What did you want to see me about?'

'You know.'

'I don't.'

'Yes, you do. I killed Elliott and Stobbs and the German boy.'

It was such a relief for the Chief Inspector to hear those words that he didn't want to do anything to interrupt the flow. 'Go on. Why did you kill them?'

'Elliot was a homosexual, you know, and wanted me to commit an offence with him. I'd seen him around in those pubs – you know, where they gather. And one night we got talking and he asked me to go with him in his car to a pub in Baslow. So I did. We'd just got into Clod Hall Lane – not where he was found, but the other end – and he stopped the car and wanted to commit the offence. I hit him on the jaw. I hate things like that, I really do. I wanted to kill him. I got a stone from the wall and hit him with it. Then I loaded the body into the car and dumped it at the other end of the lane. I drove back in the car, parked it while I got some fish and chips, then left it in Park Road.'

'Did the same thing happen with Stobbs?'

'More or less, yes. I met him in the same pub. He spoke to me, and I knew he was one of those. I hate them, and I decided to kill him. It was my idea to go to Stubbing Court. We left the car by the stream and had a walk round. Then I hit him with a hammer. I dragged the body back to the car and dumped it in Clod Hall Lane again. I had a few bloodstains on my suit but I washed them off.'

'What about the German boy?'

'I'm really sorry about that one. That was really brutal. I didn't even know who he was. They were making love, you see, like I've seen my mother do many times. I hated them for it. I followed them and stabbed him. I don't know how many times. I just kept stabbing. While I was doing it I accidentally stabbed myself in the leg.'

'Would you like to make a statement about all this, Michael? Really get it off your chest?'

'No. I can't make a statement. It would only make trouble for my family.'

He was kept at the police station all night but still refused to make a statement and claimed that if he was charged he would deny everything. They let him go. On Friday 11 December 1964 he was finally charged with the three murders.*

Copeland was brought to trial at Birmingham Assizes on Wednesday 17 March 1965 before Mr Justice Ashworth. Graham Swanwick QC prosecuted, and Copeland was defended by Rudolph Lyons QC.

His story was that, to end the intolerable surveillance,

---

* In 1964, the Offences Against the Person Act gave British courts jurisdiction in cases of murder committed abroad by British subjects.

he had forced the police to charge him, by making false confessions, which he would afterwards be able to deny successfully. But the jury took three hours to decide that in his confessions Copeland had shown that he knew too much of the murders to deny them convincingly, and they brought in a verdict of 'guilty' on each of the three charges of murder. He was given the death sentence but, since the law on capital punishment was at that time under review, he was automatically reprieved and the sentence changed to life imprisonment.

12   Pascoe and Whitty:
The Miser's Hoard

'That's the second time tonight,' complained the pillion passenger as the motorcycle spluttered to a halt. His thin fair hair was blowing in the wind. He wasn't wearing a crash helmet, for this was an August night in 1963, and in those days wearing a helmet was not compulsory. Not that he would have worn one anyway. He was not a young man who took kindly to rules and regulations.

The driver wearily got off the machine. 'Put a sock in it, will you? You've done nothing but complain since we started.' He was a stocky, powerful young man, with curly black hair and a swarthy complexion. He leaned over to adjust the carburettor while his passenger got off to stretch his legs.

'How much further is it?'

'Not very far. Just the other side of Constantine.'

The fair young man knew that his friend had been raised in the village of Constantine, some seven miles from Falmouth, in Cornwall.

'Know this place well?'

'Nanjarrow Farm? Course I do. Worked there for two or three years when I left school. Old Willy Rowe's a funny character. Did you know he was a deserter in the First

World War? And his family kept him holed up in the farmhouse for forty years. You'd never credit it, would you? Never let on to anyone in the village that he was there.'

'What happened?'

'Well, his father and eldest brother died eventually and the youngest married a girl in Helston and went there to live. That left only Willy and his mother at home. When she died, four years ago, who should pop up at the funeral but Willy, who everyone had thought had been killed in the war.'

'All right, all right. Spare me all the family history. The important thing is, has he got plenty of money?'

'He's loaded. Doesn't believe in banks. (Mind you, few of them do around here.) Never spends anything if he can help it. He must have thousands stashed away in that old farmhouse.'

'And all we've got to do is to relieve him of it,' chuckled the fair young man.

'It'll be easy. A few years ago another chap and I burgled the place one day when old Willy was out in the fields. We found over £300. But my so-called mate cleared off with most of it.'

He switched on, hoisted a leg over the bike and kicked the starter pedal. The engine coughed uncertainly into life. He revved up. 'Get on,' he said to his passenger. 'Have you got the tools?'

The fair young man patted his pocket in which he carried an iron bar about a foot long, a sheath knife and a starting-pistol. He was wearing a blue blazer with brass buttons which he had borrowed from a girl, and the driver had a pair of white gloves which he had also borrowed from a ladyfriend.

'Here's what we'll do,' said the driver. 'We'll stop a fair distance away, so he won't hear the engine, and walk from there.'

They continued their journey.

Some time later they arrived at the back door of the farmhouse, which was set in rolling hills near the village of Constantine. The front door was never used – in fact, it was nailed shut, as were all the windows. The sixty-four-year-old Willy Rowe had a fear of the house being broken into. As a consequence he never slept upstairs, but on a settee in the downstairs kitchen. He ate off a table in the same room, and by his side was a shotgun which had been there so long it had worn a groove in the table top. It was going to be no easy job to pry Willy Rowe loose from his money.

But the two young men had a plan. The fair one with the smart blue blazer knocked, while his friend, who would have been recognized if he'd been seen, concealed himself in the shadows by the side of the door.

A rough voice answered from inside: 'What do you want?'

'Excuse me, sir, but I'm a helicopter pilot. I've just crash-landed in one of your fields. I wondered if I could ring for assistance?'

This was not such a wild idea as it may sound, for the previous February a helicopter from the Royal Naval Air Service station at Culdrose had indeed crashed nearby and one of the crew, who had broken his ankle, had actually been allowed inside the farmhouse to rest while waiting for the ambulance.

There was silence for a while as Willy Rowe digested this information. Finally the muffled voice came again. 'I haven't got a phone.'

'Oh, that's very unfortunate. I really must get to a phone. Can you tell me where the nearest one is?'

There were muttered imprecations from the other side of the shuttered door and after a long pause the sound of bolts being withdrawn. The door opened a crack.

'It's just down the road.'

'Which way is that, sir? You see, I'm a stranger to the district.'

'You can't miss it.' Willy Rowe peered out and saw a fair-haired young man who was unknown to him. It was then that he made his big mistake. He decided that the lad looked all right. Muttering and grumbling, he eased himself through the doorway. 'I'll just point the way, that's all.'

The short and unkempt figure of the farmer carried a lantern in one hand and a shotgun in the other and wafted forwards an unpleasant smell, for he had never been known to take a bath.

Willy Rowe didn't see the young man carrying an iron bar in his hand who came up behind him.

The following morning, Thursday 15 August 1963, an agricultural salesman arrived at Nanjarrow Farm. He knew how things were with Willy Rowe and therefore drove his car round to the back and stopped in the gateway leading to the cobblestone yard. After trying for some time to make someone hear in the house, he began a search for the old man.

He found the stretched-out figure of the farmer lying face down near a drain where slaughtered beasts were bled. Willy Rowe was dead.

The salesman called the police, and the same day the Chief Constable of Cornwall, R.B. Matthews, got in touch with Scotland Yard. As a result Detective Superintendent Maurice Osborn of D Division and Detective Sergeant Andrew McPhee caught the midnight train from Paddington to Falmouth.

The post-mortem, conducted the next day by the County Pathologist, Dr F.D.M. Hocking, revealed that the farmer had been beaten about the head with a blunt instrument, the blows having fractured the skull. In addition he had received five stab wounds in the chest, two in the neck and one across the right ear. The top portion of the third finger of the left hand was also severed, presumably while the old man was trying to protect himself from the knife.

Superintendent Osborn, after going to the scene of the

crime and to the post-mortem, called a press conference. Giving details of the murder, he mentioned that death was caused by head injuries inflicted by a blunt instrument, but he made no mention of the stab wounds.

After the conference he considered the possibilities. The nature of the injuries had convinced Dr Hocking that the stabbing and the blows to the head had all been inflicted at about the same time. This indicated that the attack had been made by two people, one wielding a knife, the other the blunt instrument.

'It looks very much to me,' said the Superintendent to Detective Sergeant McPhee, 'as if we are looking for a couple of local men. Only locals would have been able to make their way to the place in the dark. They must have heard rumours that the old man kept money hidden in the house. I'll have a word with the senior officers in the local constabularies, get them to think up names of local tearaways and criminals. You can begin to make a list of people, anyone who would be likely to know of old man Rowe and his money and who'd not be adverse to a spot of thieving – because this may have been a robbery which simply went wrong.'

Later that same day the Superintendent was approached by a Detective Sergeant from the Falmouth Police. The Sergeant was well known for his extensive knowledge of the local people.

'If I could add a name to your list, sir?'

'By all means, Sergeant.'

'There's a lad called Russell Pascoe, who comes from Constantine, the village quite near Nanjarrow Farm. In fact, his parents still live there.'

'And he would know about Willy Rowe?'

'Undoubtedly, and about the thousands of pounds he's reputed to have hidden in the farmhouse. I believe he used to work for the old man at one time.'

'Sounds like a possibility. Any form?'

'We've never been able to pin anything on him, but he's

been suspected of a number of break-ins in cafés along the coast. Old Man Rowe himself suspected him of being involved when his place was robbed a couple of years ago.'

'It sounds to me, Sergeant, as if this lad Pascoe should go fairly high on the list. I'll see him this evening.'

'There's more, sir. Pascoe has a friend, Dennis Whitty, about the same age, early twenties. Although Pascoe is married and has a child, he lives with this Dennis Whitty in a caravan at the Kenwyn Caravan Park at Truro, which is only a matter of thirteen or fourteen miles from Constantine. It's a scandal in the area, as they have two, if not three, girls living with them.'

Superintendent Osborn telephoned the Truro Police and asked them to go to the caravan, and Superintendent Keast and a Detective Constable duly knocked on the door of the caravan at the Kenwyn Caravan Park. It was opened by a smallish young man with fair hair thinning on top.

'Are you Russell Pascoe?' asked the Superintendent.

'No, I'm Dennis Whitty. Pascoe's gone to see his mother in Constantine.'

There were two girls in the caravan with Whitty, Susan and Linda – these are not their real names. They were all three taken to Truro Police Station.

It transpired that there were three girls living in the caravan with the two men. Susan, who was nineteen, slept with Whitty, while the other two, who were both twenty, shared a bed with Pascoe. The third girl will be called Christine, though this is not her real name.

Linda and Christine had both been in trouble with the police. Linda had been put on probation in 1961 for obtaining credit by fraud, and Christine had been sent to Borstal for a similar offence.

When Susan, who had been living in the caravan for only a week, was interviewed by Superintendent Osborn, she claimed that the two young men had been in all that particular evening.

'Neither of them went out that night,' she said.

'What about Pascoe? You sleep with Whitty, don't you? You would have noticed if he'd got up in the night and gone out. But what about Pascoe?'

There was a long pause. Then Susan said slowly, 'It's possible I wouldn't have known.'

'And you haven't seen him with any implements?'

'Implements?'

'Things with which the murder was committed.'

'I've not seen him with a knife or anything like that.'

'Susan, how did you know the murder was done with a knife? I've never mentioned it. And it wasn't in the papers. Only the murderer could have known that Mr Rowe was stabbed.'

The girl's face went white.

This was the breakthrough the Superintendent had been waiting for, and soon after that Susan admitted everything.

She said she'd seen the two men go out at about half-past ten on Pascoe's motorcycle and return at one o'clock in the morning. Whitty seemed particularly quiet when he came to bed, and she asked him what was the matter. He told her there had been some trouble that night and that a farmer had been stabbed.

The other two girls eventually corroborated the story. Linda said she had been out on the afternoon following and had bought a paper which reported the murder at Constantine. Knowing that the two men had been there the previous night, she asked Whitty if he had been involved in the murder. He said he had. Pascoe came in soon after and confirmed that he too had taken part. But he threatened the girls that the same thing would happen to them if they said anything to the police.

Pascoe was picked up at Constantine and taken to Falmouth Police Station. Faced with the girls' statements, the two young men soon confessed to the crime. But each blamed the other for the actual murder.

Pascoe claimed that he had struck the old man only once, hitting him over the head with the iron bar merely to knock him out. Then, according to him, Whitty had seized the bar from him and continued to belabour the old man about the head with it, and finally stabbed him with the knife.

Whitty agreed that he had stabbed Rowe, but only, he said, because he was forced to by Pascoe, of whom he was afraid. And he said he had never used the iron bar at all.

Their trial began at the Cornwall Assizes, held at Bodmin on Tuesday 29 October 1963, and ended on the following Saturday. Mr Justice Thesiger presided, and Norman Brodick QC prosecuted. Whitty was defended by Norman Skelhorn QC, Pascoe by J.P. Comyn QC.

The charge was 'murder in the furtherance of theft', which in those days carried the death penalty. Both Skelhorn and Comyn tried to get the jury to reduce the charge to one of manslaughter. Skelhorn, for Whitty, submitted that there was a case for diminished responsibility, since there was some evidence that he had suffered blackouts and had been threatened by Pascoe. But the jury disagreed and brought in verdicts of 'guilty' against each man. The two young men were hanged on Christmas Eve 1963.

The proceeds of the robbery, for which these two were prepared to commit murder, turned out to be very small: £4 in money, which they found hidden under a piano, some boxes of matches and two old watches worth only a few pounds each. The old farmhouse had kept its secrets from the two intruders.

And it looked as if that farmhouse, which had kept its secret of the existence of the deserter Willy Rowe for forty years, was going to keep the secret of where the money was hidden. Although the police made an intensive search of the premises, they discovered only £20 in silver, stuffed into jamjars and hidden at the back of an old stove.

The place was not easy to search. The whole house was

in a shocking mess, looking as if the occupant had never done any cleaning at all. It had no gas, electricity or piped water. The only water came from a well in the yard.

The police did find, on the table where the farmer ate his meals, a pile of *Teach Yourself* language books – it looked as if Willy used to study them in the evenings. Some time later an exercise book with his handwriting was discovered at the back of an old bureau. It was written in a mixture of Spanish and Esperanto and contained maps and diagrams which looked as if they referred to places on the eighty-acre farm.

One spot which was marked in the exercise book appeared to be in one of the cowsheds. When the floor was dug up, three feet down the door of an old safe was discovered, facing upwards. In another place in the same cowshed, and also indicated in the book, the keys to the safe were found. And when it was opened, the safe proved to contain a large sum in cash in old £5 notes.

Fields were referred to in the book in terms of their old names, and in the corner of one digging unearthed an old wine bottle, then another and another. Scores were eventually found. Each had been carefully corked and sealed and then thrust, neck first, into jamjars filled with grease. And each bottle contained carefully rolled banknotes. There were literally thousands of pounds buried in this way, which had it not been for the murder, would never have been discovered – not for hundreds of years anyway.

13 Raymond Morris: The Missing Hours

The man in the grey car was on his way home from work. It was a warm Saturday, 19 August 1967, and Corporation Street, near the centre of the small Midland town of Walsall, was crowded with cars and lorries. Through a break in the traffic up ahead, the man saw three children about to cross the road from the opposite side. He was middle-aged, an experienced driver, and he slowed down, preparing to brake suddenly should the children rush out into the street.

They were about seven or eight years old, two boys and a little girl. The girl was wearing a pale, short-sleeved shirt, long trousers and black plimsolls. She had straight, dark hair cut in a fringe at the front and coming down over her ears and, as she turned to and fro, looking for a space in the traffic, her dark, glossy hair swung out from her head like a halo.

The man's heart missed a beat.

Then the children crossed, disappearing behind the lorry in front and reappearing on the pavement to his left. He edged his car forwards slowly. They were laughing and joking and pushing each other about the pavement, and he had a sudden fear that the boys would push the girl into the road. Then they went down the side turning he knew to be Camden Street.

The man in the grey car looked quickly in his mirror, flicked his indicator to turn left, swung the wheel.

The three children were a few yards down the street, just passing some factory gates. He drew up behind them and leaned across to wind down his window. The trio had stopped and were looking curiously at him.

'Excuse me. Which way is it to Caldmore Green?'

He pronounced it 'Karmer Green', so the boy whose name was Nicholas Baldry knew that the man was local.

'It's just up there,' said Nicholas, pointing back the way they had come. 'Round to the right.'

The man opened his car door. Ignoring the boys, he said: 'You look a clever little girl to me. Are you going to hop in and show me the way?' The little girl hesitated. 'Hurry up,' said the man. 'If you're a good girl and show me the way properly, I'll buy you some sweets to take back to your friends.' He pushed the car door open wider. 'You two boys stay here, and wait for her. We shan't be a minute.'

The little girl, whose name was Christine Darby, got into the car, and the door slammed shut behind her. It was 2.30 p.m.

Nicholas Baldry, who'd had his eighth birthday only a fortnight before, was a bright boy. They'd all been warned at school not to go with strangers, and he was not happy about Christine's getting in the car, but it had happened so quickly that he'd not been able to think of anything to say. He stood watching the car as it turned round and went back up the street. When it reached the main road, instead of turning right, it turned left, and he knew then that something was wrong.

He raced down Camden Street to number 80, where young Christine lived with her mother and grandparents, and banged on the door. It was opened by the little girl's grandmother, and Nicholas burst out with his story. Her mother, Mrs Lillian Darby, soon came to the door, and the two women rushed to a nearby off-licence, where there was a phone, to make a 999 call.

Both women were very worried, because in the past couple of years there had been two other cases in the area of little girls who had gone missing. They were Margaret Reynolds of Aston, a suburb of Birmingham, and Diane Tift of Bloxwich, a small town just north of Walsall. The girls had eventually been found murdered on Cannock Chase, a region of woodland and open ground some hundred square miles in extent and thirteen miles north of Walsall.

By soon after three o'clock on that Saturday afternoon road blocks had been set up around the town, and hundreds of motorists were stopped and questioned and their cars searched. But it soon became obvious that the grey car and its occupants had slipped through the net. House-to-house enquiries were begun in Camden Street, and policemen were drafted out to search Mansty Gulley, the spot on Cannock Chase where the bodies of the two little girls had previously been found. But by the end of that day there were no clues to the whereabouts of Christine Darby.

The next day the house-to-house enquiries continued. Posters, with a photograph of Christine and the words 'Did You See This Girl?' were printed and put in prominent places in the town. Waste ground, parks and open spaces of all kinds were searched.

And then, late on that Sunday evening, a mounted policeman searching part of the Chase found a pair of child's knickers by the side of the Rugeley to Penkridge road. The next day they were identified as Christine Darby's by her grandmother, who recognized some stitching she had done on one of the legs.

It was the first positive indication of the fate which had overtaken the small child. There were soon to be others.

On Monday 400 police officers from forces throughout

the Midlands began a search of Cannock Chase. They were joined by 700 troops. Later in the day, a black plimsoll was discovered by a woodman some three miles from where the knickers had been found. It was hung on a tree and looked as if it might have been flung from a car. The signs were ominous.

Scotland Yard were called in, and on Tuesday Detective Superintendent Ian Forbes and his assistant, Detective Sergeant Thomas Parry, joined the team. The search concentrated on the area where the plimsoll had been found. At 2 p.m. police frogmen began a search of flooded gravel pits nearby, and lines of soldiers began moving, shoulder to shoulder, across the ground, beating the fern-covered undergrowth and searching beneath the trees.

At 5.40 p.m. a soldier saw what looked like crumpled clothing partly hidden by the bracken and ferns. It was the body of little Christine Darby, wearing only her shirt, slip and white socks. Now it was officially a murder case and, since the body had been discovered near the A34 trunk road, it became known as 'the A34 Murder'.

An incident room had already been established in the small town of Cannock, just to the south of Cannock Chase, and this became the headquarters in the hunt for the killer. It was linked by radio and closed-circuit television to the incident room at Walsall Police Headquarters, and it was at Cannock that the massive filing system, which was to run into many thousands of entries, was installed. Every telephone call, interview and enquiry was carefully logged, indexed and cross-referenced.

Dr Alan Usher, Home Office Pathologist, reported that the little girl had been suffocated to death. By the bruising to the face it was most likely that this had been done by a hand across the nose and mouth, and the pathologist gave it as his opinion that Christine had died during the course of a ferocious sexual assault at the place where she was found. Her body had been torn, and there was a great deal of blood on her and on the ground.

Dr Usher put the time of death as late Saturday or early Sunday, and the police put out a call for anyone who had been on the Chase on Saturday afternoon or evening or Sunday morning to come forward.

Eventually they were successful. Victor Whitehouse had been exercising his dog on Cannock Chase that Saturday afternoon in an area where plantations of trees were divided by wide firebreaks. As he was walking along one of these, he noticed a car parked not in the firebreak but in a narrow 'ride' which went off at right angles. It was unusual to see cars parked in these rides as there wasn't enough room to turn a car round in them. The vehicle was a grey colour, and he thought it was an Austin A60. The driver's door was open, and there was a man standing behind the door. He looked to be middle-aged, with dark hair. It was about four o'clock in the afternoon.

The place where Mr Whitehouse saw the man was only a few yards from where the body of Christine Darby was subsequently discovered.

At about 4.20 the same afternoon a Mr and Mrs Rawlings were driving on the Chase with their dog. They stopped their car and, while Mr Rawlings was putting on his rubber boots, Mrs Rawlings was getting the dog out. A car rushed past, quite close to where she was standing. It was a grey Austin Cambridge, she thought, and the driver was a dark-haired man. He was alone in the vehicle.

Both Mr Whitehouse and Mrs Rawlings were able to give descriptions of the man, and from these an Identikit picture was made and published in the local newspapers, placed on hoardings and broadcast on television.

At the same time a massive hunt was launched for the grey car. Detective Superintendent Ian Forbes, the burly Scotsman in charge of the murder investigation, addressed key members of his team:

'The man we're looking for is probably local, and he

drives a grey Austin A55 or A60. To make sure he doesn't slip through our fingers, we're going to check every grey car in the Midlands.'

There was a whistle of astonishment from the assembled police officers.

Forbes continued: 'We'll be going to every taxation office and searching their files to locate the owners of every grey or near-grey car, and then we'll interview everyone.'

In all, the police examined nearly 1½ million taxation files and by February the following year, six months after the murder, had interviewed over 23,000 car-owners. But they had not been able to identify the murderer.

'We've just got too many suspects,' said Detective Sergeant Parry to his boss. 'We've got dozens of people with the right sort of car and who more or less fit the description, but they've all got alibis.'

'I'm convinced he's a Walsall man,' said the Detective Superintendent. 'We'll do another house-to-house in the Walsall area. We'll really take this place apart. Somebody must know something they're not telling us!'

And so yet another investigation was launched. Nearly 40,000 homes were visited, and some 28,000 men interviewed. Some were seen several times. But by the end of the search the police were still no further forward. So the effort was scaled down, the investigation went on hold, and Forbes and Parry went back to London.

It wasn't until the following November that there was a further twist in the story. It came on 4th of that month, the evening before Bonfire Night, in Bridgeman Street, which is not very far from Camden Street, where Christine Darby had been abducted. On some waste ground there a ten-year-old girl and her brother were building a bonfire for the following night. It was about a quarter to eight and already dark when a man approached the little girl.

'Do you want some fireworks?' The two children looked at him suspiciously. 'I've bought some for my little boy, but now he's going to a firework party and doesn't need them.' The man looked at their suspicious faces. 'But if you don't want them, I'll soon find someone who does.' He turned away.

'Just a minute, mister,' said the little boy.

But his sister cut in: 'You know we're not supposed to talk to strangers!'

'Quite right,' said the man. Then addressing the little boy: 'Your friend here is more sensible than you are. You shouldn't talk to strange people in the street. But in this case it doesn't matter because I'm not going to offer to take you anywhere. All I'm going to do is to give you some fireworks. That's if you want them. It's OK with me if you don't. I'll give them to somebody else.'

'I suppose it's all right,' said the little girl doubtfully, 'if you just want to give us some.'

'Up to you,' said the man. 'I've got the fireworks in the car over there,' he pointed across the road to the Bridgeman Street Garage. 'You can come and get them if you like.'

The little girl hesitated a second, then nodded. She followed him as he turned and walked across the road. It was brightly lit by the street lamps, and she could see his car standing on the garage forecourt a few yards away.

The man went to the driver's door and unlocked it, then turned as the little girl came up. He took hold of her arm.

But the child was not intimidated by the big man beside her. She looked through the car window. 'There's no fireworks in there!' she snapped.

'Yes, there is. They're round the other side, on the passenger seat.' He pulled her arm to lead her round the other side.

But the little girl was not convinced. She suddenly stepped back and, with surprising strength, jerked her arm free, then turned and fled across the road. The man stood and watched her. For a moment it seemed as if he was contemplating following. Then he opened the car door and got in.

If the man had driven off quickly, the Christine Darby case might still be a mystery, and people might today still be speculating as to who, out of the thousands of car-drivers in the Midlands, was the murderer. But he didn't. Instead he sat in the driver's seat and for a few minutes, in either remorse or frustration, rested his head on the steering-wheel. This gave the young woman who had just come out of a fish shop across the road and who had seen everything time to note the number of the car.

The young woman quickly got in touch with the police. A message was passed to Scotland Yard, and in the meantime the local police began enquiries about the owner of the car the woman had seen and which she described as being a green Ford Corsair with a white top.

When Forbes and Parry arrived at the incident room a few days later, they were met by Detective Chief Superintendent Harry Bailey, Head of the Staffordshire CID, who had been in charge of the case while Forbes was in London. Bailey had a long face.

'Not good news?' enquired the Scotland Yard detective.

'Good and bad,' replied the Staffordshire man. 'The first thing we found was that the number which the woman gave us, LOP 429, is not the number of a Ford Corsair at all. It belongs to a car in Yorkshire and is obviously nothing to do with the case.'

'Are the registration letters local?' asked Forbes.

'In this area,' confirmed Bailey. 'They're a Birmingham registration. So we guessed that she'd got the letters right but had made a mistake about the numbers. The first number, we've found, is often given correctly by eye-witnesses, but they make mistakes about the following numbers. So we tried transposing the figures, and our first attempt hit the jackpot. LOP 492 is in fact the number of a Spruce Green Ford Corsair with a cream top. And it's owned by a local man.'

'That's great!' said Forbes joyfully.

But Bailey shook his head. 'We've had him in for

interviews and an identification parade but, though he hasn't got much of an alibi, neither the woman nor the children could identify him, so we've had to let him go.'

'Hmm,' said Forbes. 'Do you think he's our man?'

'He's our man, all right. He's had this green Corsair only a couple of months. Before that he had a grey Austin Cambridge.'

'What's his name?'

'Raymond Leslie Morris. Lives only just across the road from the West Midlands Police Headquarters in Walsall.'

'I remember him,' said Sergeant Parry, the man who had set up the massive filing system which had been one of the features of the case – and a man with an encyclopaedic memory. 'He was one of our original suspects, but he was alibied by his wife, wasn't he?'

'That's right,' replied Bailey. 'He was interviewed twice if not three times in the investigation. He's employed in Oldbury, about six or seven miles south of Walsall, as works foreman at an engineering factory. On the Saturday Christine Darby was killed, he clocked out at 1.13 p.m., though he claims he didn't leave the works until 1.30 because he had to wait to hand over to the owner, who had been away on holiday. He then drove home in his grey Austin A55. He claims he didn't go through the centre of Walsall but went round on the ring road. But he could just as easily have gone up through the town and in that case would have passed the end of Camden Street where little Christine was picked up. He lives on the fourth floor of a block of council flats in Green Lane, and he says he got home at between two o'clock and 2.15. And his wife confirms this. According to him, they went shopping in Walsall at about 4.30 and then went on to visit his mother-in-law. And this is supported by his wife.'

'Hmm,' said Forbes again. 'What about the Identikit picture? Does it look like him?'

'Well, you know what these things are like,' replied Bailey. 'It could well be him, but I wouldn't like to swear that it's a perfect likeness.'

'I think we'd better have him in again. And I'll see his wife,' said the Scotland Yard man.

On Friday 15 November Raymond Morris was picked up by the police while on his way to work and taken to Stafford Police Station.

His wife, Carol, worked as a clerk for a firm in Walsall. She was seen at work the same day and taken to the police station at Hednesford. There she was interviewed by Superintendent Forbes. Looking at the documents relating to her, he noted that she was twenty-six years old, some fourteen years younger than her husband, and they had been married three years.

'I just want to confirm your evidence concerning your husband,' he said, looking again at his notes. 'You were both seen on two occasions in September 1967, just after the Christine Darby murder, and once in February 1968?'

Carol Morris nodded her head. 'I think that's right,' she muttered.

'Just tell me again what time your husband got home that Saturday afternoon.'

Mrs Morris repeated that her husband had come home from work at 1.30 p.m. He had behaved quite normally, stripping to the waist and washing in the kitchen, as he always did, and then having a meal. At about 4.30 they had gone shopping in Walsall. She was taken over the story, backwards and forwards, over and over again by relays of policemen, but she never deviated from it in the slightest. This went on for several hours.

Eventually Forbes confronted her again. 'Mrs Morris,' he said, 'we're not getting anywhere here, are we?'

She said nothing.

'Mrs Morris,' he said again, but this time casually, idly tapping with a pencil on the table in front of him, 'You might think that, because this was such a terrible crime, the murder of a wee child, the man who did it must be some kind of monster, easily recognizable as such.' He looked across the table at her and shook his head. 'It's just not so. I've met quite a few murderers of this kind, and most were very ordinary men. The sort of man I might meet at a football match. The sort of man you might see going round the stores on a Saturday doing the weekly shopping.'

He looked across at her but could see that her face was still set. 'Most of these men are apparently very fond of children,' he said quietly. 'See a young girl and this man is the first to bounce her on his knee, laughing and joking with the child.'

'And I suppose every man who makes a fuss of children is a potential sex maniac? Is that what you mean?'

'Obviously not,' he said quietly. 'All I'm saying is that the murderer would behave like this. He'll always be the one to buy children sweets and presents. He'll help with dressing them. He might even offer to put them to bed.'

Forbes looked across at Mrs Morris. Her face hadn't changed, and she still sat in the same tense position, but he had a feeling that something had changed in her. Something he'd said had struck a chord somewhere. He left her alone to think about the situation.

Sometime later they were again sitting facing each other. Forbes shuffled the papers before him on the table. 'Now, Mrs Morris, this is a very serious business, and the time has come for the truth.' He took a deep breath. 'What time did your husband get home on Saturday 19 August last year?'

There was silence for a long time, and then the young woman said, in a voice so low that it could hardly be heard: '4.30. He said he'd been kept late at work.'

When Raymond Morris was brought to trial at Staffordshire Assizes on Monday 10 February 1969, before Mr Justice Ashworth, the evidence brought by the prosecuting counsel, Brian Gibbens, QC was overwhelming. Mr Whitehouse identified Morris as the man he had seen standing by the car on Cannock Chase. Mrs

Rawlings said he was the man who had driven past her on that fateful Saturday afternoon. And when Mrs Morris went into the witness box, her husband's alibi was gone. Morris was found guilty of the murder of Christine Darby and was sentenced to life imprisonment.

Some evidence which must have strongly affected the jury, and which the defending counsel rightly maintained afterwards might have swayed them against his client, was some photographs. Morris was a keen photographer, and a search of his flat after he had been arrested revealed, hidden in a sweet tin, a set of pornographic prints. They had been taken of a five-year-old girl who had stayed with the Morrises during the summer of 1968. It was quite clear that Carol Morris had no idea what was going on, but perhaps a partial realization, when she was being questioned, induced her to tell the truth about what time her husband came home.

Bibliography

Bibliography

Bresler, Fenton, *Scales of Justice* (Weidenfeld & Nicolson, 1973)

Butler, Ivan, *Murderers' England* (Robert Hale, 1973)

Capstick, J., *Given in Evidence* (John Long, 1960)

Forbes, Ian, *Squad Man* (W.H. Allen, 1973)

Furneaux, Rupert, *Famous Criminal Cases 2* (Allen Wingate, 1955)

Gaute, J.H.H., and Odell, Robin, *The Murderers' Who's Who* (Geo. G. Harrap, 1979)

Hastings, Macdonald, *The Other Mr Churchill* (Geo. G. Harrap, 1963)

Hastings, Sir Patrick, *Cases in Court* (Heinemann, 1949)

Hastings, Patricia, *The Life of Patrick Hastings* (The Cresset Press, 1959)

Hawkes, Harry, *Murder on the A34* (John Long, 1970)

Hugget, R., and Berry, P., *Daughters of Cain* (George Allen and Unwin, 1956)

Humphreys, Christmas, *Seven Murderers* (Heinemann, 1931)

Jackson, Sir Richard, *Occupied With Crime* (Geo. G. Harrap, 1967)

McKnight, Gerald, *The Murder Squad* (W.H. Allen, 1967)

Montgomery Hyde, H., *Norman Birkett* (Hamish Hamilton, 1964)

Rowland, J., *Poisoner in the Dock* (Arco Publications, 1960)

Sanders, Bruce, *Murder in Lonely Places* (Herbert Jenkins, 1960)

Wild, Rowland, *Crimes and Cases of 1933* (Rich and Cowan, 1934)

Wilson, Patrick, *Children Who Kill* (Michael Joseph, 1973)
Murderess (Michael Joseph, 1971)

The files of the *Birmingham Evening Mail, Carmarthen Journal, Derbyshire Times, Eastbourne Chronicle, Eastbourne Gazette, Glossopdale Chronicle, Horncastle News, Huddersfield Daily Examiner, Lincolnshire Chronicle, Lincolnshire Echo, Manchester Evening Chronicle, Manchester Evening News, News of the World, Oldham Evening Chronicle, The People, Peterborough Citizen and Advertiser, Poole and Dorset Herald, Sunday Chronicle, South Wales Argus, South Wales Evening Post, West Briton and Cornwall Advertiser, Yorkshire Post.*

Index

Index